The Art of
Extreme Wig Styling

Regan Cerato
of Cowbutt Crunchies Cosplay

FanPOwered
PRESS
an imprint of C&T Publishing

Text and photography copyright © 2021 by Regan Cerato

Publisher: Amy Barrett-Daffin

Creative Director: Gailen Runge

Acquisitions Editor: Roxane Cerda

Managing Editor: Liz Aneloski

Cover Designers: Regan Cerato and April Mostek

Book Designer: Regan Cerato

Production Coordinator: Zinnia Heinzmann

Production Editor: Jennifer Warren

Illustrator: Regan Cerato

Photo Assistant: Gabriel Martinez

Models: Alchemical Cosplay (page 42), Commiaownist Cosplay (page 43), Giraffe Cosplay (page 81), Ilabelle Cosplay (back cover and page 22), Pitchfork Cosplay (pages 90 and 99), and Turnfolio Cosplay (pages 8 and 56)

Cover photography by Sam Saturn

Photography by Regan Cerato, unless otherwise noted below

Additional photography copyright © Alexandra Lee Studios (pages 16, 80, and 103), Sam Saturn (cover and pages 3, 7, 8, 17, 27, 42, 43, 55, 56, 58, 81, 84, 87, 90, 93, and 99), and Sorario Days (back cover and pages 6, 22, 70, and 96)

Library of Congress Control Number: 2021934039

Printed in the USA
10 9 8 7 6 5 4 3 2 1

Acknowledgments

Dedicated to the inspiring Ila, and to Sam, Theresa, and Alex who are always encouraging me to conquer bigger and bolder things!

With special thanks to our friends for all of their support: Eric, Pearl, Emilia, TJ, Cat, Carrie, Ian, Zach, Matt, Lauren, Jacqui, Jenna, Paul, Tyler, Kayla, Rob, Hope, Tuan, Dan, Mary, Sarah, Alex, Amanda, Beverly, Luisa, Lizz, Daisy, Maggie, and Marlowe.

And to my copy editors Pitchforkcosplay, Ryephoenix, Elephantbird Cosplay, Shieldivarius, Sweetlyneurotic, Mhysarose, and Banaheif.

Thank you to our patreons for their support!

Abi, Alex Young, Alexis Davis, Alexis Dinsdale, Allison Reid, Allyson Bode, Amanda Rodriguez, Amanda Sako, Anna Thuesen, April Davis, Ashleigh, Banaheif, Bigimotik Cosplay, Black Cat, Brianna, Bridgette Leon, Bridie Damisch, Brigitte Quinn, Brittany Waddy, Brodie Williams, Caileesi Cosplay, Caroline Seidman, Cat Wei, Celine Thermann, Christine Geiger, Cinderkitten, Claudia Gilman, Cortnee Jarvis, Courtney Stewart, Cynix, Denise Chukhina, Distorted Echo, Elephantbird Cosplay, Emily Rabener DVM, Emissary of Wind, Ena, Francine Lassen, Freeda_M, Gus McGrath, Heather, Intrepid_Canvas, Jamie, Janelle Jensen, Jenna Say What, Jessica Hustace, Jessica Lipsius, Jessica Luna Cosplay, Jessica Robyn, John Hetherington, Joyce Hsu, Kaimitsu, Katie F, Katie Starer, Katie Wicker, Kellyn Morrow , Kristin Benini, Lauren Olivier, Lauren Venezia , Lucas Johnson, Lynzie Dugar, Maia Weithington, Mariecarmen Ruiz Lundberg, Meghan Perry, Midnight Post, Mikomi Hokina, Mina Henderson, Miss Madison Cosplay, Morgan, Nanashi, Nathalie Molly Shawn, nekomiminechan, Nicole Wilson, Niho Palaoa, nooglenol, P T, Rebecca Partin, Rebecca Ramsey, RR, Sam Blalock , Samantha Ruffin, Sarah Stalcup, Sedinam Gadzekpo, Soulirus, Stefania Sharp, Steff Von Schweetz, Stormy Douglas, Surya, swagyatta, Tawny Owl, Taylor Porter, Tiana, Tundabolt, Ugly Snail, Valencia Cook, Valerie Martinez, Vic, Yandere Kevinn, Zachary Eckert, Zack Doe

Contents

Let's Make Some Wigs!

Welcome, stylists! I am one-half of Cowbutt Crunchies Cosplay, and for years I've loved creating everything from giant ballgowns to detailed armor. Larger-than-life wigs are a specialty of mine, but over the years I've found that extravagant wigs can be intimidating for even the most seasoned of crafters. However, I believe that extreme wig making is for everybody: anyone from beginner to advanced stylist can tackle these styles with a combination of the right techniques, patience, and ambition!

This book includes many of my favorite styling methods and tips that I've picked up over the years, as well as several of my own wig creations to serve as artistic inspiration. I've also included a hefty number of guides on both essential and extreme styling techniques, along with a number of talking points on best practices, tips, and instructions for re-creating common styles. My teaching style centers around stepping readers through the logic behind why exactly a styling technique works. I want you to walk away with knowledge that you can apply to your own future projects beyond what's contained in this book. Use these chapters as a guideline, but as always there is no one "right" way to style—be sure to try new things, experiment, and adopt the techniques that work best for you!

Working with wigs in general, and especially making larger-than-life wigs, inherently involves working with a lot of synthetic materials, tools, and chemicals. Always work in a well-ventilated space, and always read and follow all safety instructions for the products you choose to use.

SECTION I
FOUNDATIONS

CHAPTER

THE BUILDING BLOCKS OF WIGS

01

Wig Terminology

Wig

1. Wig Cap
2. Netting
3. Crown
4. Ear Tab
5. Elastic Band
6. Adjustable Strap
7. Weft

Weft

1. Weft Track
2. Stitch Line
3. Hair Fiber
4. Fiber Ends

Fiber Contents

What are synthetic wigs made of?

Most synthetic wig fiber is composed of long strings of plastic. Unlike the keratin in human hair, plastic is shinier, often thicker, and can withstand more abuse. There are many different types of wig fiber plastic out there, and some brands even use their own special blends. Extremely cheap "bag wigs" that you might see in a Halloween store have a tell-tale shine that indicates that the fiber is made of low-quality plastic. Older brands and "ready-wear" wigs tend to be made of Kanekalon fibers, which can vary in shine and come in limited, more realistic colors like blondes and browns. This can be great if you're looking for realistic hair tones, but bear in mind that some wigs like this are not heat resistant. They cannot accept very hot temperatures from tools like flat irons (up to 400 degrees F), and may melt under an extremely hot blow dryer. Keep an eye out for wigs that are labeled as "heat resistant" and especially ones that come in a variety of colors and thicknesses. Depending on which store you purchase your wig from, you may notice that your fiber might have a slick sheen to it or that it might appear almost matte. This is due to the blend of fiber used.

Matte fiber versus slick fiber

All fibers are not created equally! While I am a firm believer that you can style any wig with enough effort, I also believe that there is always a way to make less work for yourself. Matte fibers tend to be thicker and coarser, while slicker or shiny fiber tends to be thinner and smoother.

Aside from a personal visual preference, this has a few important effects on our styling. Coarse fibers like those sold by cosplay brands Arda Wigs or The Five Wits naturally have more "tooth" to them and tend to grab onto each other even with natural wear. This is a great advantage and can save effort when you need to tease or spike a wig. However, for this same reason long styles made with matte fiber tend to tangle more with wear and friction.

To contrast, if your wig displays a visible shine or sheen, it may be made from thinner, softer wig hair. These fibers tend to slide against each other rather than knot and tangle. A good rule of thumb is to use slicker fiber if you want a long wig that doesn't tangle as easily. Or if you need a shorter wig with lots of upward volume, matte fiber will help you achieve that look.

> TIP: Don't want to follow the above suggestion? That's fine too: pick the fiber type you like best!
>
> If using matte fiber for a long wig, be sure to apply a detangling spray before wearing. If using slick fiber for heavy styling, a few sprays of hairspray will give the hair some temporary grip during the teasing process.

Wig Styling Tools

Essential Styling Tools

Below is a list of go-to tools that I keep in my styling arsenal. Wig styling is possible with any number of tools, but if you're looking for a place to begin building a collection, these are my personal favorites.

❶ Canvas Wig Head and Stand
Canvas wig heads are more expensive than Styrofoam heads, but they are larger and a better match for a human head's dimensions. This becomes very important when eyeballing the general shape or size of what you are styling.

❷ Blow Dryer
Applying heat from a blow dryer is essential to soften plastic fibers during the styling process.

❸ göt2b Freeze Spray
göt2b (by Schwarzkopf), an extremely heavy-duty hairspray, is a favorite of cosplayers everywhere due to its strong hold that behaves like a mix of hairspray and glue.

❹ Wig Scissors
You don't need to run to the bank for these since plastic wig fiber will quickly dull any blade, but pick up an inexpensive pair of cutting shears if you can. You'll find cutting far less frustrating if you use these instead of craft scissors.

⑤ Flat Iron

For heat-resistant wigs, a flat iron supplies more heat than a blow dryer and is great for straightening, curling, and teasing wigs.

⑥ Fine Toothed Comb

Cleanliness is king, so use a fine toothed comb to ensure that all of your fibers are straight and untangled.

⑦ Wide Toothed Comb

If your wig is tangled or needs to be combed for flyaways, start with a wide toothed comb instead.

⑧ Tacky Glue or PVA Glue

White, flexible glues are readily accessible and great for styles built up with foam.

⑨ Teasing Brush

This is a dense-bristled brush designed for teasing. It does a great job of teasing large quantities of hair fast. It's also fantastic for smoothing out just the top layer of hair without disturbing the teased layers.

⑩ Duckbill Clips

Solid metal duckbill clips are my favorites for clipping aside pieces of hair. They're strong and don't cause tangles.

⑪ Detangling Spray

Detangling sprays contain oil, which will slicken wig fibers. Mist your wig with this spray to prevent tangling during normal wear or to assist with unknotting a tangled wig.

Additional Styling Tools

① Steamer

A handheld steamer is a great way to apply a large amount of heat when curling or smoothing out hair.

② Spray Bottle

Combing a wig can result in static electricity. If this happens to you, spray a small amount of water on the fibers to neutralize the effect.

③ göt2b Spiking Glue

This is a washable alternative to tacky glue if you want to create super pointy spiked tips.

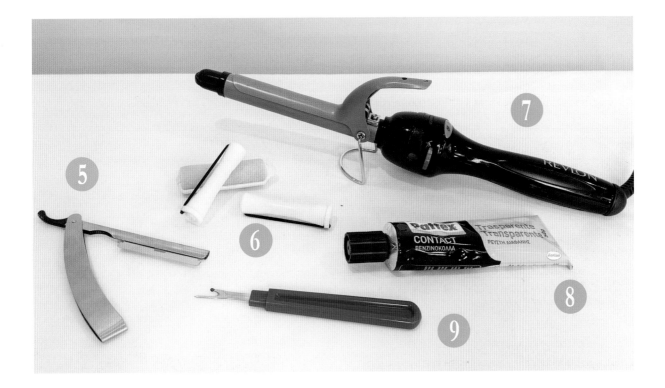

④ Butterfly Clips
These clips are great for pinning aside large quantities of hair.

⑤ Razor Comb or Razor Blade
A razor comb or a razor blade is a great timesaver and learning tool if you're new to trimming. This comb shaves away fibers at varying lengths, and can help give a more natural, tapered finish to your trims.

⑥ Curlers
If you need to curl a wig, curlers are one helpful way to do so. Any type of curler is useful, but if you regularly curl with hot water, look for plastic curlers that will retain less moisture.

⑦ Curling Iron
While a curling iron is traditionally used to heat fibers, I prefer to heat the hair using a different tool and then use a cool iron to shape fibers into ringlets.

⑧ Alternative Glues
Hot glue, Pattex Contact Adhesive, and other alternative glues can round out your wig tool arsenal. Each of these glues is useful for different styling techniques. Experiment to see which type you prefer.

⑨ Seam Ripper
This is a useful tool to have when de-wefting or rearranging wefts, as it provides easy access to tiny weft stitches.

Choosing a Glue for Your Project

It's always worth noting that there is not one "best" glue to use when styling a wig, only favorites. Personal preference is a big part of this: many stylists prefer different glue types depending on their consistency, holding power, and what type of wig they are making. I always keep several different glues on hand in my own arsenal, as I find that certain glues work best with certain projects. Whichever glue or adhesive you choose to use, be sure to work in a well-ventilated area and follow all of the safety instructions included in the product packaging.

White PVA Glue or Tacky Glue

(Clear, flexible glue)

Clear or white PVA glues are permanent unless soaked in water. This type of glue is most useful for structures that you want to remain clean and long-lasting. These glues are a great way to obtain perfectly pointy spikes; however, be aware that they can darken your fiber very slightly. They are also great glues to use for glued foamwork styles in order to create a strong, permanent shape. A correctly glued wig should maintain its form for years.

PVA glues are manufactured under many different brand names including Aleene's Original Tacky Glue and Elmer's Glue-All. Your available PVA glue may vary depending on where you live, and some may begin with a thicker consistency or have less holding power. I often use tacky glue and thin it with water, adding a few drops until it reaches the consistency of thick pancake batter. This is an important step, as otherwise the glue will be too thick to glide through the fiber. If working on your project for a long time, remember to rehydrate your glue as the water evaporates. Tacky glue will thicken and begin to dry within several minutes, so try not to finagle with your work after this drying phase has begun. Combing or picking at drying PVA glue will result in pilling and white chunks of glue. If this happens you may try rehydrating the glue, or alternatively wait until your work is fully dry and color over any visible flecks with matching markers or paint.

göt2b Freeze Spray

(Hairspray)

göt2b is my favorite general "glue" and a standard in the cosplay community. A combination of glue and hairspray, it has a nice, stiff hold that's great for spikes, teasing, and more natural-looking hairstyles. It dries quick and hard provided you hit it with a blow dryer! göt2b is fairly strong but will eventually wilt under extreme heat and long wear, so be prepared for touch ups.

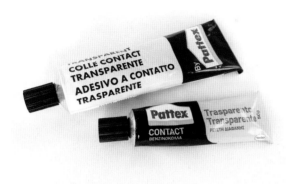

Pattex Contact Adhesive

(Clear, flexible glue)

Pattex Contact Adhesive (by Henkel) has a gel-like consistency and a potent odor. Be sure to read all safety information in the product packaging. The gel texture means it spreads easily—even better than watered down tacky glue. It is even more transparent than PVA glues, and dried glue pilling is easily smoothed away by applying additional Pattex Contact Adhesive. It's a permanent glue that can soak through all fibers, and thus is another great option for spike tips or permanent foamwork. Pattex Contact Adhesive dries significantly faster than PVA Glue, which is both a blessing and a curse. If you're a fast worker or creating smaller permanent pieces, Pattex Contact Adhesive is a great option. But with only a few minutes of working time, it may dry too quickly for larger pieces or longer hair. Pattex Contact Adhesive may also be difficult to obtain in some countries, so I tend to only use it for special projects or small pieces.

Hot Glue

(Strong, permanent glue)

Hot glue is a great option when an extremely strong hold is needed. It's secure, dries fast, and can coat every single strand, which is very important for pinning down the end of your weft. However, hot glue is visible and potentially messy. As such, it's a great tool whenever attaching points that will be hidden from view, such as a foam piece. When wrapping hair around a foam understructure, I will also often use hot glue to anchor wefts to the foam. These anchor points are hidden from view underneath the foam or behind subsequent layers of hair, where strength is more important than cleanliness.

In a pinch, hot glue can also be used when wefting hair—just be sure to avoid burns and to take extra care to keep your work clean!

A quick word about adhesive sprays

I sometimes receive questions about whether I use adhesive sprays on my wigs, and the answer is not anymore. Adhesive sprays are fast and easy to use, which can be tempting if you're under a time crunch or if you're a beginner stylist who is struggling to get their fiber to lie flat. However, sprayed fiber cannot be adjusted, and most sprays will result in white flecks of glue in your wig fiber. I do not recommend adhesive sprays if you want to take the time to work clean. But, if you're a beginner who just wants to cut their teeth on foam, or you're having a difficult time sticking your first layer of fiber to your understructure, adhesive spray could be a good learning glue for you. Just wean yourself off of it quickly!

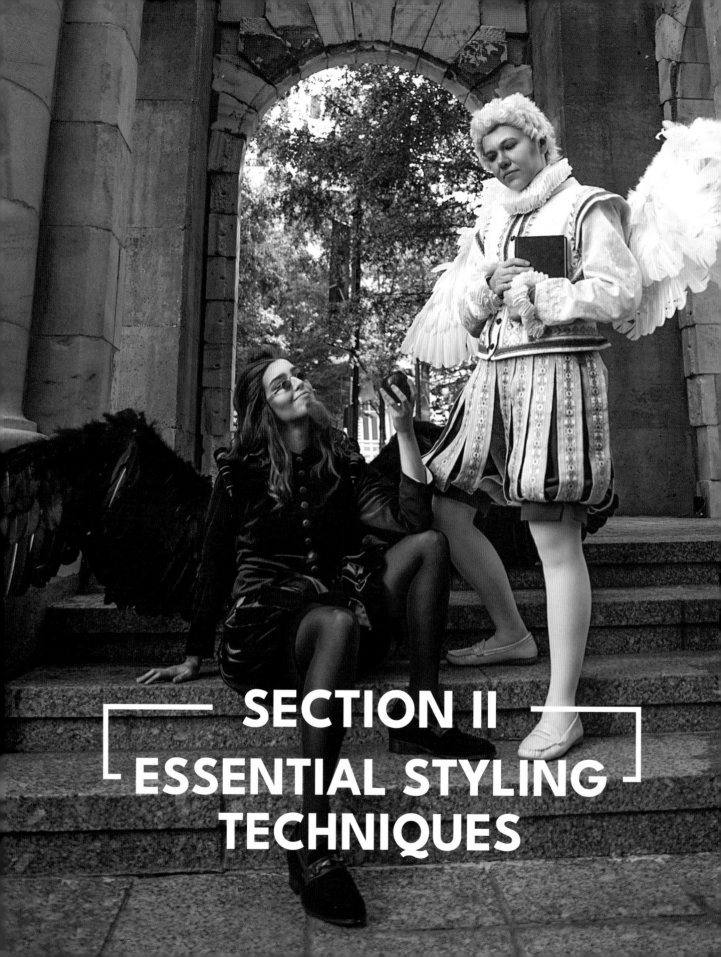

SECTION II
ESSENTIAL STYLING TECHNIQUES

02
TRIMMING TIPS

Before Beginning:
What is a "blunt cut?"

A "blunt cut" is what I call a trim where all of the hair is exactly even. While a perfectly horizontal cut like this can work on human hair, with wigs it looks odd because of the sheer amount of fiber in a wig. Too much hair on the tips of a wig will stack against itself, causing strange, rectangular bunching. This can happen with both long and short straight wigs, or even "spiked" wigs where the tips have not been appropriately feathered.

This is a "blunt cut." There are very few wig styles where this is appropriate.

Instead, the tips of your wig should look feathered, with the fibers' edges falling at different lengths. The height and amount of this feathering will affect how tapered the wig looks. For a precise, crisp cut or bob, use a short taper. For long wigs, a thinner, gradual feathering will look more natural.

Avoiding a blunt cut has everything to do with your cutting technique, and there are several tools that can assist with these cuts.

Notice how this cut is straight but still looks natural due to the feathering.

Cutting with Razors

For beginners or stylists who are not confident in their scissor skills, a razor is a great tool for your arsenal. Straight razors or razor combs are also incredibly speedy for quick styling or if you need to chop off a large quantity of hair. For extra safety look for a razor comb; this tool is constructed from a razor blade safely embedded behind a comb's teeth. This allows you to evenly comb through your hair as you feather it, while also preventing you from accidentally cutting yourself with the blade. As the razor skims over the wig fiber, it cuts away only some of the hair, which results in feathering. The harder you press with your blade, the more hair you'll cut away.

Always keep a box of replacement blades on hand, as razor combs dull extremely quickly, sometimes in the middle of cutting a single wig. The tension from snapping the fiber with a dull blade often results in twisted or curled hair toward the crown of the wig. Be sure to fix this by running a fine toothed comb through the hair, and try to smooth those tangles throughout the cutting process in order to avoid accidentally damaging the hair while combing. If you find yourself exerting more pressure on the razor because the blade no longer glides through the fiber, it's time to swap out or sharpen your blade.

Cutting Instructions

① Grab a small portion of hair and then hold on to the bottom of the fiber.

② Drag your razor over the hair, starting at the point where you'd like the hair to be shortest and ending where you'd like it to be longest. Press down with a light to moderate pressure as you drag the comb downward. Do not press too hard or you'll risk chopping off too much fiber.

③ Use a fine toothed comb to smooth out any kinked fibers.

④ Repeat several times until all hair has been trimmed.

Cutting with Scissors: Flicking Motions

For both precise control and speed, cutting shears are an excellent alternative to razor combs. This method requires flicking your wrist up and down, and during the cutting process you will never fully close the shears. Instead, the sharp edge of the blade drags along the hair, occasionally catching and cutting some fiber. We are producing a similar result to dragging a razor comb along the hair, but with a gentler, more controlled motion; a small amount of fiber is cut in random places with each drag of the shears. This can be a tough technique to get the hang of, but it's my personal favorite when it comes to trimming and long, natural feathering. Be sure to purchase a pair of sharp hair cutting shears beforehand. Expensive scissors are not necessary, but they must be sharp!

Cutting Instructions

① To begin, separate a small portion of hair. I like to hold on to the bottom tips of the fiber for a more controlled cut, but this is not necessary.

② Hold your blades perpendicular to the hair.

③ Flick your hand in an up-and-down motion at the wrist. This movement will cause the scissor blades to slide up and down along the fiber. The highest point your scissors reach will become the start of the feathered area, whereas the bottom point will become where the longest hair ends.

④ As the scissors slide against the hair, the blades will randomly trim away some fiber. Ideally your shears should be sharp enough to cut the hair by simply sliding against the fiber. However, if they are not quite sharp enough for this, you can help the process by gently opening and then halfway closing the blades, trimming a small amount of hair.

⑤ Pause when necessary to remove any cut or kinked hair with a fine toothed comb, and continue for the entire wig.

Cutting with Scissors: Angled Cutting

Angled cutting is a far slower technique but will yield more precise results! It is particularly useful on thinner areas of hair such as bangs, for crisp styles where only a small amount of feathering is needed such as bobs, or in cases where precision is required such as the tips of spikes. Angled cutting can be used on thicker wigs but will require some patience.

Cutting Instructions

① Take a portion of your hair and spread it out thinly between your fingers. This step is crucial or else you may end up with blunt cuts.

② Angle your scissors so that the tips are pointed directly upward, and then tilt them very slightly off to one side.

③ Cut into your hair. The extremely thin arrangement of hair ensures you don't cut a chunk of hair in the same spot to the same length.

④ Continue cutting along the edge of your hair, occasionally pausing to remove any stray pieces with a fine toothed comb.

TIP: If your wig looks a little too flat for your liking, try curling your edges slightly for a more natural look. Use a flat iron or blow dryer to heat the bottom half-inch of your wig. Curl the tips of the hair toward the wig head with your fingers and hold until cool. Brush out slightly to relax the curl.

CHAPTER

WORKING WITH HEAT

03

Like other thermoplastics, wig fiber will soften and become malleable when exposed to heat, which is why tools like a blow dryer or flat iron are essential when it comes to altering wigs. Nearly every styling technique takes advantage of this heating trick. Physically changing the shape of your wig fibers will help your styling last longer than it might with only glue or pins. Remember that under extreme heat plastic can also melt. Using a heat gun instead of a blow dryer or placing your blow dryer directly against a wig that's not heat resistant can result in crimped fiber or solid lumps of plastic.

Heat Styling Basics:

In general, basic heat styling will always follow these core steps:

① Apply heat to the area you would like to style. If using a blow dryer, hold the nozzle at least several inches away and heat the area consistently. If using a flat iron for even higher heat, quickly swipe the iron over the strands 1–3 times until the fiber is fully heated. Don't hover too long in one area or else you risk crimping the fibers.

② Hold your hair in the new, desired direction. Use your hands, bobby pins, or clips to hold the hair in place, but do not release the hair while it is still warm and malleable. Unlike human hair, synthetic fiber will not solidify into a new shape until it is cool.

③ Release the hair only once the fiber has completely cooled.

④ Spray with hairspray or göt2b Freeze Spray. To immediately harden and set your göt2b Freeze Spray, run your blow dryer over that area for several seconds.

Heat Styling Basics: Straightening

A flat iron makes quick work of straightening hair, especially for longer wigs. To soften curls or create a wavy style, use a blow dryer instead as this will produce less heat.

① Prep your workspace. If straightening an entire wig, save time by using gravity to your advantage: place your wig on its wig stand and allow the fiber to hang downward.

② Separate a chunk of fiber from the wig.

③ Swipe your flat iron over the full length of the fiber, pulling down slightly as you go. Repeat this process again until the fiber is warmed.

④ If using a blow dryer, heat the strand evenly. If working with a long wig, try working in sections, heating a portion of the hair at a time.

⑤ Working quickly, take a fine toothed comb and swipe it downward. This will help the fiber separate and droop toward the floor.

⑥ Repeat for all necessary areas of the wig.

Heat Styling Basics: Curling

Curling with a flat iron

This option gives you a great amount of control over where your curls lie and their tightness. While time-intensive, you can easily correct any mistakes since you are curling each individual piece of hair.

① Separate a half-handful of fiber from the wig.

② Swipe your flat iron over the hair several times until it's very hot.

③ Moving quickly, curl the hair from tip to root around a cool curling iron. If you do not have a curling iron on hand you can use any sort of cylindrical item like a brush handle or a pen for extra small curls. For extremely tiny pin curls, you can even twist the hair with your fingers.

④ Hold the hair in place until it cools completely.

⑤ Unwrap the hair and spritz with göt2b Freeze Spray or hairspray.

⑥ Repeat for the remainder of the wig.

Curling with hair curlers

An alternative option is to curl your entire wig at once using extreme amounts of heat for very tight curls. This option may save you some time but requires extra supplies. For best results, use wire cage curlers and a steamer; this combination allows the heat to penetrate all of the fiber layers. If you do not have a steamer available, hot water will also provide a large amount of heat. However, work carefully with the hot water method—dunking your wig can cause tangles and the entire wig must be curled at once.

① Begin wrapping your wig's hair around hair curlers. While any kind of curler will work with the hot water method, steam will permeate caged curlers best. Sponge rollers will also take significantly longer to dry.

② Continue until your entire wig is wrapped in curlers.

If using a steamer:

③ Heat your steamer and apply a generous amount of steam to each roller. Always hold the steamer by the handle and never put your fingers near hot steam.

④ Allow the wig to completely cool.

⑤ Remove the rollers and spritz with göt2b Freeze Spray.

If using hot water:

③ Heat a pot of water to near-boiling.

④ Place the wig in a bathtub and pour your water over the top of the wig. If you are using a large enough pot, you may also dunk the wig directly into the water. Take care to avoid any hot steam while handling the pot.

⑤ Hang the wig in a safe space or place it back on your wig head. Once completely dry, remove the rollers and spritz with göt2b Freeze Spray.

Heat Styling Basics: Extra Lift

Does your wig need a touch more volume or require hair that points upward? Applying only heat is a great way to achieve a more "natural" looking style.

① Hold your wig upside down and shake it out slightly.

② Blow dry your wig, evenly heating the fibers until they are warm to the touch.

③ Shake the wig out again and use your fingers to help the fibers droop toward the floor.

④ Spritz with hairspray and allow to cool in this upside down position.

⑤ Turn your wig right side up and evaluate your poof. Repeat the above steps as necessary for more volume, or for less volume gently smooth the hair down with your hands.

Heat Styling Basics: Less Poof

Sometimes a wig can have too much lift. If that's the case, use these steps to flatten your wig around the crown area.

① Place your wig on its wig stand.

② Run a fine toothed comb through the wig, focusing on the crown. If this area is teased, try to untangle or flatten the hair as much as possible.

③ Blow dry your wig from the top down, heating the fibers until they are warm to the touch.

④ The air blast from the dryer should have already pushed your fibers downward, but push down with your hand if you need the hair to flatten even more.

⑤ Allow to cool and spritz with hairspray.

Heat Styling Basics: Hair Flips

① Blow dry the area to be flipped, evenly heating until the fibers are warm to the touch. Alternatively, swipe your flat iron over the area. You want a fair amount of heat for this step.

② Hold the hair around a large cylindrical object such as a soda can. Depending on how long your wig is, you can even use your hands to form the curled shape.

③ Hold the hair in its curled shape until it has completely cooled.

④ Spritz with göt2b Freeze Spray or hairspray to help lock in the shape.

DYEING WIGS

04

Having trouble finding the right wig in the color you need? Custom coloring might be the best route to take if you cannot find the correct combination, if your favorite wig supplier doesn't carry your needed color, or if your wig requires more than one shade. There are several different methods for coloring a wig, and which one you choose depends on the type of color you need as well as the end results you are looking for. Finally, how you color a wig can also boil down to personal preference. Some people prefer the quick, fast color of polyester dye, while others prefer the control and cleanliness of markers!

Wig Coloring Basics

Wig Coloring Basics

Remember that wigs are composed of plastic fiber! Hair dye created for keratin in human hair will not cling to your wig; instead wigs should be dyed with materials that are formulated to tint plastic. This includes polyester fabric dyes, sharpies, high-quality artist markers, and some types of ink or diluted paint. Some materials work better than others and some have different levels of difficulty involved. All tints however are what I would refer to as "mostly" permanent. Depending on your color, you will most likely experience some level of bleed after you finish coloring your wig. Most bleeding can be prevented by very thoroughly washing your wig in warm water with soap. However, some dyes may continue to run in the rain or against the friction of a costume's collar even after washing. While this is an extreme situation, it is a huge disadvantage to dyeing if it's imperative that your wig not bleed at all!

Should I color my wig?

Coloring a wig can be messy, finicky, and time-consuming. If possible, I always recommend taking the extra time to find a wig in the right shade. If the correct color and style combination cannot be found, you may still wish to purchase the correct color in the wrong style to then cut later. However, if you struggle with any sort of styling but enjoy dyeing, you may prefer the opposite. Your mileage will also vary depending on the coloring method you use.

TIP: Dye can only darken or enhance your wig's color; it is not possible to lighten a dark wig. You can however over-dye a colored wig in order to blend colors and achieve a new tone. For instance, adding blue to a pink wig will create a lavender color.

Dyeing with Polyester Fabric Dye

Pros:

- Extremely rich, dark colors
- Easy to mix colors
- Very fast
- Dye is inexpensive

Cons:

- Requires separate equipment investment
- Requires ventilation and safety precautions
- Dye colors may be limited or will require mix tests
- Wigs must be restyled
- Long wigs may severely tangle
- Prone to bleeding without thorough washing

A bold, saturated color is a perfect candidate for fabric dye

Best for: short, richly colored wigs

For short, bold-colored wigs that you don't mind restyling, fabric dye is a great option! This is often my go-to for dyeing because an entire wig can be dyed in just five minutes and the color will always turn out extremely rich and bold. That's the fastest option you're going to get!

However, the downside to using dye comes with the prep and clean up. Dye can give off fumes and so you must be sure to ventilate the area you're working in. Polyester dye must also be heated to near-simmering in a pot that is not used for food. Finally, dropping a wig in very hot water will soften the fibers so any previous style will immediately be gone once you pull it out of the water. This can be a nightmare for long wigs or wefts, which will badly tangle in the water. You can use this method to dye long wigs if you are careful, but anticipate spending a good amount of time detangling and straightening your wig.

Remember to make sure you have selected a dye formulated specifically for polyester. Natural dyes will not stick to plastic and will not affect your wig's color tone. Two popular polyester dyes in the cosplay

community are iDye Poly (by Jacquard Products) or Rit DyeMore, both of which make excellent choices. Whichever dye you choose for your project, be sure to read and follow all of the safety instructions included in the product packaging.

Polyester dye only activates at higher temperatures, so it's important to keep the water at or just below simmering to achieve dark tones. At simmering temperatures, wig fiber absorbs dye very quickly. If you need a pastel or lighter tone and a quick 10-second dunk is too difficult, try adding significantly less dye or try turning the heat down to prevent adhesion.

The following dye tests utilized three brands of pure white fiber from Arda Wigs, Epic Cosplay, and an alternative brand L-email Wig. Each absorbed the dye in a similar way, and each looked nearly indistinguishable after the dye bath. We could see some slight variation when placed under a scanner, but this should not discourage you from attempting to dye your favorite brands. Polyester dye works great on all synthetic fibers.

iDye Poly Color Chart

White wig fiber in ⅛ tsp (1ml) dye and 1 cup (250ml) water, heated to simmering unless otherwise stated

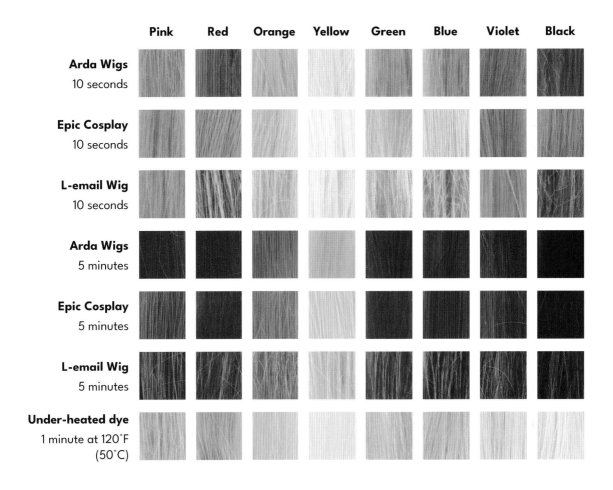

iDye Poly comes in a sealed, dissolvable powder packet. This dye is easy to use since you can easily toss the entire container into your water. However, it's much harder to partition out portions of dye for color mixing or to save for later. To save your dye powder, snip open the packet corner and empty the powder into a plastic bag. During my tests I found that iDye was more potent than Rit for some tones, but was more difficult to wash from the fiber and required significantly more ventilation.

For the above color tests I used ⅛ tsp (1ml) iDye Poly, heated to just under simmering (180 degrees F [85 degrees C]) with the exception of the bottom row that was under-heated to only 120 degrees F (50 degrees C).

Rit DyeMore Color Chart

White wig fiber in 1 tsp (5ml) dye and 1 cup (250ml) water, heated to simmering unless otherwise stated

	Super Pink	Racing Red	Apricot Orange	Daffodil Yellow	Peacock Green	Sapphire Blue	Royal Purple	Graphite *4 tsp (20ml)
Arda Wigs 10 seconds								
Epic Cosplay 10 seconds								
L-email Wig 10 seconds								
Arda Wigs 5 minutes								
Epic Cosplay 5 minutes								
L-email Wig 5 minutes								
Under-heated dye 1 minute at 120°F (50°C)								

Rit DyeMore is a liquid-form dye that comes in a bottle, which is easy to mix and save for later. During my tests we found that Rit was far less smelly than iDye Poly. However, Rit's black and darker tones required significantly more dye in order to achieve a deep color.

For the above color tests I used 2 cups (500 ml) of water with 1 tsp (5ml) Rit DyeMore with the exception of the Graphite tests, which required 4 tsp (20ml) of dye. The dye bath was heated to just under simmering (180 degrees F [85 degrees C]) with the exception of the bottom row that was under-heated to only 120 degrees F (50 degrees C).

Polyester Dyeing Instructions

Materials:

· Wig of choice
· Dye of choice
· A large cooking pot not used for food
· Tongs, a spoon, or dowel not used for food
· A nearby window for ventilation
· Dish soap
· Gloves and paper towels
· Flat iron and combs

① Prepare your work area and your wig. Your wig should be free of any oils or product that can interfere with the dye process, so if it has been worn before be sure to wash it in soap and water. Remember that dye is not food-safe: anything that touches your dye cannot be used later for cooking or food storage! It's a great idea to invest in a dye-only cookpot for your projects. Dye can be smelly and irritating, so be sure to open a window for ventilation, especially if you are using iDye Poly. Gloves and paper towels are also a great idea to protect your counter and hands from dye stains.

② Fill your pot with enough water to completely submerge your wig. You want your wig to be able to float freely in the pot. Wig fiber will discolor if it touches the bottom of the heated pot for too long!

TIP: Don't have a dye pot? If your fiber only needs a quick dunk, try pouring your simmering water into a different container before adding your dye and fiber. The water will still be hot enough to activate the dye.

③ Add your dye to the dye bath and thoroughly mix. Rich, deep colors require more dye, while pastels require much less than you think: as little as one-tenth of a packet or bottle. Long wigs will also require slightly more dye than short wigs as there is more fiber to color. A pack of iDye Poly or a bottle of Rit can dye up to 2lbs (1kg) of material, so consider the weight and volume of your wig when measuring out the amount of your dye. One-third or half of a pack or bottle should be sufficient for most projects; however, if attempting to achieve a very bold or dark color, always err on the side of more. Polyester dye activates at a higher temperature than natural dye. For best results, heat your dye to simmering or just below boiling, around 160–180 degrees F (70–85 degrees C). Take care to avoid any hot steam while handling the pot.

④ Perform a test with a sample weft in order to determine how long it will take to dye your wig the desired shade. Remove the weft, wash, and allow to fully dry in order to determine the sample's color.

⑤ Dampen your wig with water and then completely submerge in the dye bath. For a lighter color, remove the wig within a few seconds or under a minute. For a deeper color, keep submerged for over five minutes. Gently stir your wig in order to help the dye evenly absorb, but try not to tangle the fibers or else you'll have difficulty combing them out later.

TIP: *Having trouble quickly dunking your wig for a light tone? Try adding significantly less dye, or try turning down the heat to a cozy 120 degrees F (50 degrees C). This will allow you to keep the wig underwater for longer without darkening the color. Refer to the dye color charts (pages 30 and 31) for the approximate color you can achieve with this under-heated dye.*

⑥ Remove your wig and run it under warm water. Add soap and massage it through all fibers before running it under the water again. Repeat several times until the water runs clear.

⑦ Your wig fibers will be bent in new and fun directions thanks to the heat, so you'll need a little restyling. Allow the wig to fully dry first and then comb out any large tangles with a wide toothed comb. Once detangled, refer to Working with Heat (page 22) to return your wig to its original straight or curly style.

Dyeing with Markers

Pros:

· Inexpensive, easily available materials
· Fantastic color range
· No special equipment required
· Spray bottle coloring is fast
· Wigs will not need heavy restyling
· High coloring control
· Color may be removed

Cons:

· Some markers come in limited colors
· Most wigs will require many markers
· Time consuming to directly apply for the darkest result
· Some markers prone to bleeding without thorough washing
· May experience bleeding when hairspray or alcohol is applied

Best for: lace fronts, ombrés, or realistic colors

Alcohol-based markers such as Sharpie Markers or Copic artist markers result in less mess and more control. They are great options, but your mileage will vary depending on the product and method used. The easiest way to use a marker is to simply pop off the cap and begin coloring directly onto the wig fiber. Because both sides of every fiber must be colored, this is extremely time consuming but will result in a bold, deep color. Marker color may be removed from a wig using 91% or 99% isopropyl alcohol. Be careful when using hairsprays on a wig colored with markers: some hairsprays contain high quantities of alcohol and may result in similar bleeding or removal, especially if the wig is rubbed while wet. Always test before spraying your dyed wig with an unknown product. As with any other material you use, remember to read and follow all manufacturer safety information.

Coloring with sharpies is a beloved cosplay method because of how inexpensive and readily available these markers are. However, Sharpie Markers come in a limited color range and they are very prone to bleeding, especially if not washed thoroughly! Do not wear your wig without washing, or else the color will rub off on everything it touches. Your color may also lighten slightly with washing. Allowing the color to set for a few hours prior to washing may help.

Artist markers are far less prone to bleed than Sharpie Markers and come in the widest variety of available colors, including realistic hair tones. This makes them a great compromise between the bold colors of polyester dye and the handling ease of Sharpie Markers. High-quality artist markers can come with a high price tag, but keep an eye out for brands such as Copic that sell comparatively inexpensive ink refills.

Marker Coloring Instructions

Materials:

· Wig of choice
· Marker color of choice (Be sure to pick up several or an ink refill!)
· Dish soap
· Gloves if desired
· Wig head (optional)

① Select your marker and then place your wig against a firm surface, such as a wig head or a piece of cardboard.

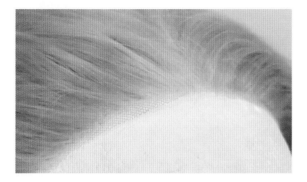

② Press your marker tip against the wig and begin coloring directly on the wig fibers.

③ Once you have fully tinted a portion of hair, flip 1–2 of those colored wefts to expose a new area of uncolored hair. Swipe your marker over the back of the tinted fiber if any of the original color is still visible.

④ Begin coloring this newly exposed area of uncolored wig fiber.

⑤ Repeat steps 2–4 until the entire wig has been tinted.

⑥ Wait for several hours and then thoroughly wash the wig in warm water with soap.

A faster way to color with markers is to create a dye bath using 70% alcohol as a diluting agent. This is a much quicker way to color your wig but typically produces lighter results because the ink is not as potent. Deeper results can be obtained but you will need to dilute your marker bath less and spray in multiple layers. For normal dyeing you will likely want at least 3–4 cores for a short wig, depending on your color.

Marker Dyeing Instructions

Materials:

· Wig of choice
· Wig head
· Marker color or ink refill of choice (Be sure to pick up several!)
· Spray bottle
· 70% isopropyl alcohol
· Dish soap
· Gloves
· Tarp, plastic bag, or newspaper

① If using a Sharpie Marker, cut open the tip of the marker with scissors and remove the ink-saturated core. If using Copic markers I highly recommend purchasing an ink refill bottle, but if only markers are available, cut open the end of the marker. Using tweezers, remove as much of the ink-soaked fiber contents as possible, along with the marker tip.

② Drop all of your marker contents from step 1 into a small spray bottle containing one cup of 70% isopropyl alcohol. For a shoulder-length wig, you will need around four markers or half a refill bottle, depending on your color. Darker colors will require more. Be sure to experiment to find the right ratio. Diluting the mixture will result in a lighter color.

③ Replace the bottle lid and allow the ink to seep out over 24 hours.

④ Cover your workspace with a tarp and then place your wig on a wig head. Begin spraying the mixture onto your wig.

⑤ When one area is saturated, clip that hair aside to expose any uncolored fibers. Spray that area and repeat until all fiber is covered

⑥ Allow several hours for the alcohol to completely evaporate and dry. If a darker color is desired, repeat steps 4–5 for a second layer.

⑦ Wash your wig thoroughly with soap and warm water to remove any excess dye. If using Sharpie Markers, repeat this bath several times.

Dyeing with Artist Inks

Pros:

· Inks are inexpensive and will cover an entire wig
· Inks are easily mixable
· Readily available materials
· Will not bleed when hairspray is applied

Cons:

· Limited color range
· Wig fibers will be stiff without washing
· Color may fade or bleed during washing

Best for: fast fixes, ombrés, or root coloring

High-quality artist inks such as Daler-Rowney FW or India ink adhere well to plastic and can also be used for wig dyeing. Inks may be diluted slightly with water and then painted directly onto a wig using a brush, which provides control and faster speed than markers. This can be ideal for roots, ombrés, or large coloring jobs. These inks are thicker than either markers or polyester dyes, so it is essential to wash your wig thoroughly after allowing the ink a full day to dry and set. Depending on your ink, this washing can cause your wig to lose much of its initial color, especially with darker or deeper tones. Try to allow as much setting time as possible to prevent this, or repeat the painting process with a second layer. Be sure to work in a well-ventilated area and to read and follow all manufacturer safety instructions.

Ink Coloring Instructions

Materials:

· Wig of choice
· Ink color of choice
· Paintbrush or spray bottle
· Bottle or jar
· Dish soap
· Tarp, plastic bag, or newspaper
· Wig head
· Gloves

① Pour your ink into a jar and dilute with water. For a pastel wig try a 1:8 ratio of water to ink. 1:4 or 1:2 may be needed for a deeper tone. The stronger the ink concentration the darker your color will be.

② Cover your workspace with a tarp and then place your wig on a wig head.

③ Dip your paintbrush into the ink mixture and begin painting directly onto the fibers. Optionally, pour your mixture into a spray bottle and spray the mixture onto the wig.

④ Once you have fully tinted a portion of hair, flip several of those colored wefts to expose a new area of uncolored hair. Paint the back of the tinted fiber if any of the original color is still visible.

⑤ Begin coloring this newly exposed area of uncolored wig fiber.

⑥ Repeat steps 2–4 until the entire wig has been tinted.

⑦ Allow the wig to dry for 24 hours and then thoroughly wash in warm water with dish soap or shampoo.

Coloring Roots

Darkening or tinting a wig's roots can give your wig additional depth and a more realistic tone. This technique is also useful for characters with unusual shades of hair. Partially coloring a wig in this manner can be tricky because it's not possible to submerge just that portion of the wig in a pot of hot water or to color only that area with a spray bottle. Fortunately, markers and inks are more precise options that allow us to tint only the root area.

① If using inks or a liquid marker mixture, prepare your mixture using the instructions in Ink Coloring Instructions (page 38) or Marker Dyeing Instructions (page 36). Select a color that is darker than your base wig.

② Part the hair and clip it aside to expose the entire weft, including the sewn line.

③ Paint your ink or press your marker directly onto the sewn edge of the weft. Add half an inch of color below this line and blend it out.

④ Clip this hair aside to expose another uncolored weft and repeat steps 2–3 for the entirety of the wig.

⑤ For additional realism, deepen some areas with a second color or a darker tone.

⑥ If coloring with inks, allow to completely dry overnight.

> TIP: If precision is key, avoid over-wetting your brush: watery ink will sometimes "creep" a very small amount down the unpainted fiber.

Ombré Dyeing

An ombré colored wig begins with one color at the crown and fades into another color closer to the bottom of the hair. Some ombré examples include a blonde wig with dark roots or a wig with red fiber near the crown and pink fiber near the tips.

Similar tones or light to dark tones

If your desired ombré requires two similar tones or light to dark tones such as a blonde to brown, pink to red, or white to green, begin with a wig in your lighter color. This method will also work if your ombré features a dark to light contrast, even if the colors are not similar, such as mint to dark brown.

Different tones

If your desired ombré requires two different tones such as blue to red or green to purple, you will need to dye both portions of the wig. For this method, begin with a white or light wig and ombré dye each side separately.

Ombré Coloring with Markers, Sharpie Markers, or Ink

While time consuming, hand coloring will give the greatest control over where your ombré fade occurs.

① Determine where you would like the color change to occur and place a clip or bobby pin in this spot to mark it. For a gradual fade, your "gradient area" will include 1 to 2 inches (2.5 to 5 centimeters) above and below this line.

② Color your wig according to Marker Coloring Instructions (page 35) or Ink Coloring Instructions (page 38) until you reach the start of the gradient area.

③ Begin coloring fewer of the strands, or use less pressure for a lighter color.

④ Continue lightening your color more and more until you reach the bottom of the gradient area.

⑤ If creating a contrasting ombré, repeat the above instructions in your second color for the opposite direction.

> TIP: *You can spray diluted marker ink for a faster but similar effect. However, watch out for accidental drips, as too much spray will cause the color to leak downward to the tips of the wig.*

Ombré Coloring with Dye

Ombré dyeing with dye will yield a bold contrast, but it can be tricky to achieve a gradual color fade in the correct spot. Harsh dye lines or accidentally adding color to the wrong place are potential mistakes to avoid.

① Determine roughly where you would like the gradient to occur. Section off unneeded hair with a large butterfly clip.

② Dip the half of your wig to be dyed into your dye bath referring to Dyeing with Polyester Fabric Dye (page 29).

③ Submerge for several sections and then slowly lift the wig 2–4 inches (5–10 centimeters) above the water, depending on how gradual you would like your gradient to be.

④ Slowly lower the wig back to its original point and lift again. Repeat this process for several minutes.

⑤ Remove from the dye bath and immediately rinse with soap and water.

⑥ If creating a contrasting ombré, allow the wig to completely dry and prepare a second dye bath for the contrasting color. Clip the dyed portion of the wig for easy handling and submerge the undyed portion of your wig up to the original dye point. Repeat the above instructions for the contrasting dye bath.

SECTION III
EXTREME STYLING TECHNIQUES

CHAPTER

05
ALL ABOUT WEFTS

Now that we've tackled our basics and essentials, it's time to move on to the world of extreme styling! An extreme wig can involve all sorts of different techniques, but these styles typically appear "larger than life." Extreme wigs require more hair than a human can grow or sometimes look as though they contain more hair than can be found within a single wig. With that in mind, the following chapters should provide you with two important takeaways when tackling extreme projects. First, it is often necessary to focus on adding large amounts of volume so you have more material to work with. Second, the key to a great permanent style is not hairspray or glue: it's a strong physical foundation. Glues provide a great secondary hold but may deteriorate. My favorite extreme techniques focus on creating a strong base layer that will keep its shape over time.

Beginning with Wefts

Weft Basics

In the world of extreme wig styling, manipulating wefts is essential. A weft is created from wig fiber that is laid in a row and then sewn together with thread to form a single strip of hair. Flip your wig inside out and you'll find many rows of these wefts stitched to the inside of your wig cap, often arranged from ear to ear or around the wig's part line. The arrangement of the wefts affects the direction the hair will fall in, and the quantity of wefts dictates how thick the wig will be. The more wefts attached to the cap, the more fiber is in the wig, and the thicker your wig becomes. Beginning with a thick wig is an easy way to guarantee success when styling a spiked or especially large hairstyle.

Some wig brands offer premade styles that are especially thick. However, an easy way to thicken any wig is to simply add more wefts. These wefts could originate from a few places:

❶ Create your own wefts

You can create your own wefts by purchasing loose wig fiber. This method is inexpensive but can be messy and time consuming, as each weft must be sewn or glued together.

❷ Buy premade wefts

Some cosplay wig suppliers sell ready-made wefts in matching colors, which makes this is an easy route if you are using one of those brands. If working with a long wig, try using premade wefts to avoid tangling.

❸ Harvest matching wefts

Wig wefts are sewn to the cap with thread and can be removed from a second wig using a seam ripper or scissors. This option will work for any wig brand, and as an added shortcut, harvested wefts come pre-trimmed and pre-feathered for you. Because the two wigs' wefts are identical, the harvested wefts will already be the same length as your base wig's wefts.

De-wefting and Harvesting Wefts

Inspect a weft that is attached to a wig and you'll find two rows of stitching. The first row holds down the fiber itself. This is not the stitching you want to remove! Removing this stitch line will cause the fiber to fall apart. Instead, remove the second line of stitching that attaches the weft to the wig cap itself. The easiest way to differentiate between these rows is to tug upward on your weft and insert your seam ripper between the weft and the wig cap. Any threads between the cap and the weft belong to this second row of stitching and can be safely removed.

Materials:

· Wig
· Wig head (optional)
· Quilting pins
· Seam ripper
· Duckbill clips

① Prep your harvest wig by placing it on a wig head or arranging it in your lap.

② Use a duckbill clip or two to clip away the hair on either side of your weft.

③ Now that your weft is exposed and easily visible, insert a seam ripper between the weft and the net. Rip away any thread stitches.

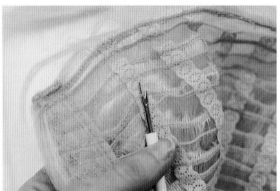

④ Begin pulling the weft away and ripping additional stitches until you reach the end of the weft. Remove it from the cap and set it aside to avoid any tangling.

> TIP: If your wig is layered, try to keep your pile of wefts in order so that you can add them to your base wig in roughly the same order.

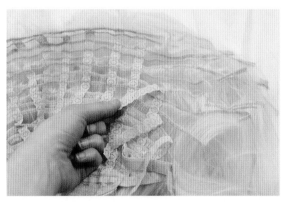

⑤ If de-wefting the entire wig, continue the above steps until you reach the wefts that are attached to the elastic bands. Insert your seam ripper between the weft and the elastic and remove any stitches.

⑥ Continue until all desired wefts have been removed.

> TIP: Did you rip a weft into two by accident? Don't panic! This is a common occurrence, and you will likely do this a few times while de-wefting. Just keep the two pieces together to later attach alongside each other.

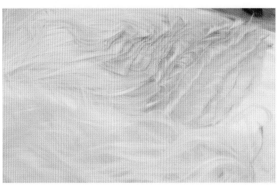

Wefting Hair

Sewn Wefts

When it comes to attaching additional wefts to a wig, sewing provides the most security but can be time consuming. This option mimics the method used by wig manufacturers and is ideal if you're concerned with permanence and stability. Sewn wefts are also visually clean and can provide a small amount of stretch, making them best for areas such as part lines or updo hairlines.

Materials:

· Wig
· Wig head
· Wefts
· Quilting pins
· Thread
· Sewing needle, either straight or curved
· Duckbill clips

① Prep your base wig by placing it on a wig head. Stretch your wig over the head and securely pin it at the front, base, and ears. If using a foam head, stretch the elastic on the sides and bottom before pinning. This is an important step, as foam heads are typically smaller than the average human head. Skipping this step may result in accidentally shrinking your wig size.

② Choose where you would like to place your weft. Use your duckbill clips to clip away the hair above this spot, exposing the empty netting.

③ Place your weft against the base wig netting. With a sewing needle or curved needle, stitch the sewn portion of the weft into the wig net using a whipstitch.

④ For the bottom half of the wig, sew your weft directly to the elastic bands.

Glued Wefts

Gluing your weft to the base cap is a great way to save time. This method is fairly secure but not as secure as a sewn weft: it is possible to rip a weft out if pulled too hard or if it was not glued properly. Do not soak a glued wig in water or fabric dye, or you will risk loosening the wefts.

Materials:

- Wig
- Wig head
- Wefts
- Tacky glue or PVA glue
- Quilting pins
- Duckbill clips

① Prep your base wig by placing it on a wig head. Stretch your wig over the head and securely pin it at the front, base, and ears. If using a foam head, stretch the elastic on the sides and bottom and then pin them so that they remain stretched.

② Choose where you would like to place your weft. Use your duckbill clips to clip away the hair above this spot, exposing the empty netting.

③ Add a thin line of tacky glue or other white PVA glue along the sewn portion of the harvested weft.

④ Place your weft against the base wig netting and push several straight pins into the weft, spacing them a half-inch apart. These pins will keep the weft pressed into the net as the glue dries, so only remove the pins after several hours.

⑤ If adding wefts to the bottom area of your wig, place a small amount of glue directly onto the elastic bands. Lay your weft on top of the glue and pin into place.

> TIP: Don't want to use PVA glue? Hot glue works great in a pinch, but this method can be messy. To avoid glue strings, add a line of glue directly to the weft and then press firmly against the netting.

Updos and Rearranging Wefts

Let's inspect our wig's wefts again. Depending on your wig style, you may find that some wefts are arranged in a circle around the crown, some lie in parallel lines between two pigtails, and others are sewn in upside down. Why do these wig styles have such dramatically different weft lines?

The direction in which the weft fiber is pointed determines the direction in which your wig's hair will naturally want to fall and where it will look the thickest. This helps the hair lie flat in the desired direction, but it also helps hide any weft tracks or netting. Pulling the hair away from its track direction can be dangerous; a small change is fine but completely reversing the direction for high pony-tails or an updo can result in exposed weft track or thinner-looking hair.

To avoid this problem, be sure to rearrange your wefts' directions when severely modifying your wig's style! Alternatively, to save time, keep an eye out for wigs that already come premade for these styles. These wigs' wefts are already arranged in the correct direction for high ponytails or reverse-wefted updos. However, you can rearrange any wig's direction by de-wefting and then re-wefting those fibers into a new track pattern.

Above shows a typical weft arrangement, while below shows a wig with perpendicular wefts for pigtails.

New Part Lines

① Place your wig on a wig head, stretch, and pin into place.

② Choose where your new part will lie and separate the hair along this line. Depending on your base wig, you may notice that large amounts of netting or elastic is exposed when the hair is pulled aside. Note how the example wig is exposed because the wefts were not arranged with a back part in mind. If this occurs with your wig, consider adding additional wefts in the following steps to hide these bare areas.

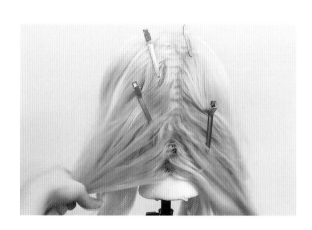

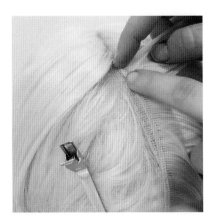  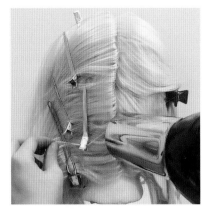

③ Lay your first weft along the center of the part line with the hair fiber pointed away from the part; in this example it is pointed toward the right side of the wig. Sew the weft into place. Sewing is recommended in order to force the weft to lie flat and straight, but glue may be used instead.

④ Lay 1–2 additional wefts on top of or to the immediate right of the first weft. Sew into place.

⑤ Fold the above wefts across the part line and toward the opposite side of the wig. In this example we are folding them toward the wig's left side. Blow dry and firmly press down.

⑥ Repeat steps 3–5 for the opposite side: add a weft to the left side of the part line with the hair fiber pointed away from the part. In this example the fiber is pointed toward the left side of the wig. Take care to place the sewn edge of the weft as close to the wefts from steps 3–5 as possible.

⑦ Lay 1–2 additional wefts on top of or to the immediate left of the above weft. Sew or glue into place.

⑧ Fold the wefts from steps 6–7 toward the opposite side of the wig to hide the weft track. Use a blow dryer to heat train this fiber flat.

> TIP: For the best results, use purchased wefts rather than harvested wefts. Purchased wefts are often thicker than layered, harvested wefts and will hide the weft's sewn areas.

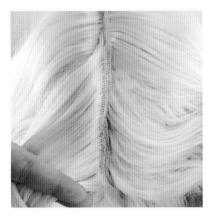  

  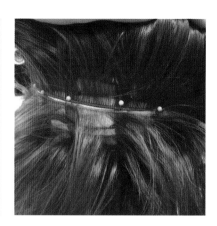

Updo Styles: Upswept Styles, High Ponytails, and Back Spikes

① Place your wig on a wig head, stretch, and pin into place.

② Remove at least half of the wefts from the back of the wig—for most wigs, this includes wefts that are attached to the elastic bands and those that lie between the ear tabs. Removing all back wefts will result in the best coverage, but only half is sufficient for many spiked styles. Keep track of which wefts belong to which part of the wig as you de-weft your fiber.

③ Place your first weft along the nape of the wig, in the same spot you removed it from. Reverse the direction of the weft fiber so that it points up toward the crown of the wig and weft into place.

④ Repeat this step until all de-wefted fiber has been added back into your wig in a reversed direction.

⑤ For a ponytail or an extreme updo, take special care to cover the base of the wig between the ear tab and the nape of the neck, as this net area is easily exposed. For these styles, obtain additional wefts or set aside 6–10 wefts from step 1 to add in later.

⑥ Arrange a weft to follow the line of the wig's edge between the ear and the wig tab at the nape of the neck, with the fiber pointed up toward the crown. Sew an additional 1–2 wefts next to this weft for additional coverage.

⑦ Stack two wefts together to create a double-thick weft. Sew these wefts to the inside edge of the wig cap with the fiber pointed downward toward the ground.

⑧ Flip the fiber around the edge of the cap and upward to hide any exposed netting.

  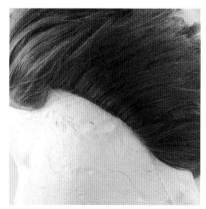

Double-Thick Wigs

Double-thick wigs are useful for all sorts of situations. They're especially great for spiked styles because of the additional volume, but they are also useful for characters with large amounts of wild, loose hair.

You can create a double-thick wig by doubling the amount of hair fiber in your base wig with additional wefts that have been purchased or harvested from a second wig. When adding this new hair, attach each fresh weft between two existing wig wefts. This will result in a pattern of old-new-old-new wefts, which will evenly distribute the new fiber throughout the wig.

> TIP: *This method works best for shorter styles or layered styles. If you do need to double weft a long wig, take care and use a generous quantity of detangling spray, as the hair will be prone to tangling.*

Our base wig's volume (*left*) vs our base wig after turning it into a double-thick wig (*right*)

Materials:

- · Base wig
- · Additional purchased wefts or a second wig
- · Wig head
- · Duckbill clips
- · Butterfly clips
- · Quilting pins
- · For sewn wefts: sewing needle and thread
- · For glued wefts: PVA glue

① Before beginning, obtain your additional set of wefts, either from purchased weft packs or via a second harvest wig. If obtaining wefts from a second wig, follow De-wefting and Harvesting Wefts (page 44) and remove all wefts from this wig. Take care to keep track of which wefts originated from which area of the wig in order to add them back in a similar spot.

② Place your base wig on a wig head, stretch, and pin into place.

③ Begin at the base of your wig and part the hair so that only the bottommost weft track is exposed. Clip the top portion of the hair out of the way.

④ Place a new weft between the bottommost weft and the weft above it. Sew or glue the weft into place referring to Wefting Hair (page 46).

⑤ Remove your duckbill clip and fold down the old weft above your newly added weft. Re-clip the hair, exposing the track line of this old weft and the netting space just above it. Add another new weft by repeating step 4.

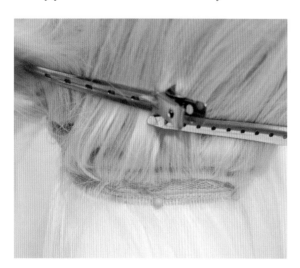

⑥ Continue re-clipping and adding new wefts every other row, working your way up toward the crown until you have added all of your wefts.

You should now have a noticeably thicker wig.

Filling In Mistakes

Even the best wig stylists make mistakes! Over-trimming an area of your wig is something that can easily happen, but don't worry—you don't necessarily have to buy a new wig. Re-wefting is a quick way to fill small mistakes by removing long wefts from one part of your wig and then moving them to an area that needs additional length. Please note that this works best with isolated mistakes rather than larger areas.

Materials:

· Your wig (optional: additional wefts)
· Wig head
· Quilting pins
· Seam ripper
· Duckbill clips
· For sewn wefts: Needle and thread
· For glued wefts: PVA glue
· Scissors

① Pin your wig to your wig head and evaluate your damage. In this example the front of our wig is several inches shorter than the rest of the wig. Because this is a small spot, we will be able to move long wefts from the back to this too-short area.

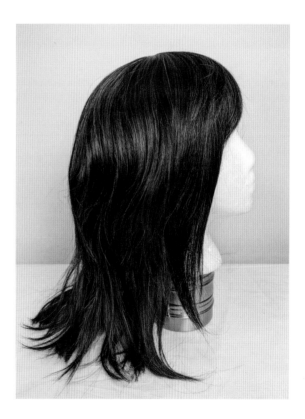

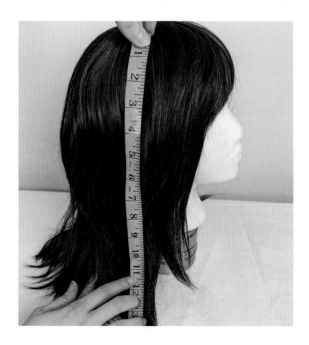

② Determine how long your replacement wefts must be. Measure from your incorrectly cut weft track to the bottom edge of where you would like your new wefts to stop. This step is important to avoid accidentally removing a weft that is too short.

③ Inspect your wig and locate the longest wefts. The longest wefts are often located toward the crown, so focus on harvesting fibers from the back of the wig at the base of this crown area. Another excellent location to harvest from is the nape of the neck. Be sure to only target wefts in areas where the hair is thickest. Removing wefts from a thin area such as a part line or the ear tabs may create netting gaps.

④ Clip back the hair above your chosen wefts. Remove the weft and repeat the process again in a different area if you need additional fiber.

⑤ Clip the hair above the damaged area and remove the problem wefts from the wig. Cut your harvested wefts into smaller strips in order to fit into your chosen space and then attach to this area.

⑥ Trim the bottom of the newly added wefts to match the length of the wig.

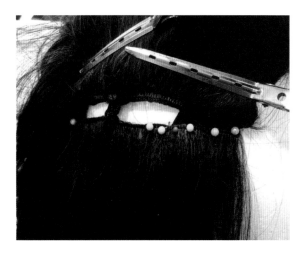

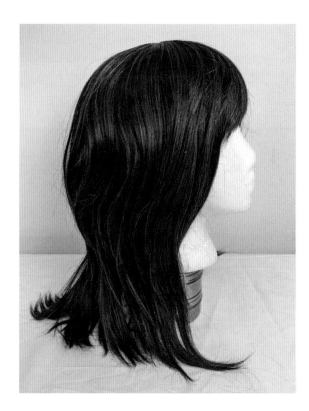

TACKLING AN EXTREME PROJECT

06

Creating Volume: All About Understructure

Does your wig require an extremely large or gravity-defying shape? Wefting in additional hair is fantastic for short wigs or as a way to create a great starting base, but wefting alone is often not enough for an extremely large style. An easy way to pad out your wig without adding weight is to add an understructure layer. An understructure is a lightweight shape that provides both extra inner volume and structural support over which to lay your wig fiber. Understructures can be made from anything lightweight but solid, and there are two primary types at your disposal.

Teasing

The first option uses teased fiber in order to add a malleable, organic understructure made from your wig's own hair. Teasing and backcombing involve tangling the wig fibers and kinking the hair so that it is no longer slick and smooth. This creates extra volume and a relatively solid shape as the fiber is knotted together. Teasing is ideal for natural curves, volume, and spikes. I find that teased wigs take on a more organic or natural quality when compared to their rigid foam counterparts, so choose this method if these qualities will be important in your finished style. Teasing is also fast and beginner-friendly if you're new to extreme styling.

Foamwork

Our second option involves creating a solid understructure from non-hair objects. Foam is the most common material used here, but this list also includes stiffened felt, batting, or poster board. Different understructures will yield different finished looks, and I enjoy using different materials depending on the wig's style. These non-hair materials can help you tackle shapes that otherwise would not be able to stand on their own such as long, flat, geometric, or extremely large shapes. Unlike teasing, which requires more fiber to create more volume and fight gravity, foam can easily double a wig's size without adding too much weight or thickness. Foam is also extremely sturdy, and a style with a foam understructure is less likely to fall apart during wear or transit.

Where to Begin

Always take a moment to form a plan of attack before starting your project. The desired shape of your wig will determine a lot about your project, including what understructure material is ideal and how to prep your base wig. Are you interested in more natural-looking, organic shapes? Teasing may be the route to go. Does your wig's geometry seem to defy logic? You'll likely want to use foamwork. Before beginning, look at your reference art and imagine a large shape underneath the wig fiber. Sketch out a simple shape, and don't be afraid to draw more than one shape if you need one. This outline will indicate the shape of the understructure you need to create.

Volumizing Cheat Sheet

Wefting

· Creates extra volume without teasing, resulting in smoother fiber

· Great for "natural" looking wigs, short wigs, or wigs with few spikes

· May not provide enough volume or holding power on its own for complex styles

Teasing

· Provides the best volume for thick spikes

· Provides additional support for long spikes

· Great for fluffy shapes, longer wigs, or curls

· Less suitable for complex or flat shapes

Foamwork

· Creates a stable, extremely resistant style

· Extremely slick and clean when formed correctly

· Great for unusual, flat, or large shapes

· Less suitable for spikes and "natural" looking styles

07
TEASING AND VOLUMIZING

Teasing Basics

Teasing serves two important purposes in wigwork. First, tangling the fibers together means that we are "locking" that hair into a new shape. This type of physical hold is extremely important when creating spikes, shapes, and other large objects that require more support than just hairspray. A physical support will always last longer than support created with hairspray or temporary glue alone. Hairspray will fade over time, but physically knotted fibers will withstand far more abuse before that style falls apart.

The second advantage we gain from teasing is increased volume, even more than we can gain from a double-thick wig. When styling an oversized shape or a head full of spikes we're looking for a large quantity of hair: something so thick and voluminous that it wants to defy gravity. This amount of volume may be an obvious requirement for fluffy shapes but it's an important key to spiked styles as well. Pinching wig fiber into a spike compresses it down, so an unusually large quantity of fiber is needed to avoid compressing spikes into thin strings.

After heating and cooling, teased hair may be combed out, but this fiber will have a noticeably kinked texture. These fibers will no longer lie flat against each other, which instead creates large open spaces and fluffy volume.

More teasing will result in more volume, but be careful not to over-tease a wig unless you plan to hide that kinked texture by other means. Instead, consider beginning with a double-thick wig base, which will provide additional starting volume and more hair to work with.

The volume of an unteased spike (*top photo*) vs a teased spike (*bottom photo*)

Basic Teasing Tips

Materials:

· Wig hair
· Teasing comb or teasing brush
· Blow dryer or flat iron

① If your hair is slick or you need help teasing, spritz your hair with hairspray to give it additional "tooth." If you are still having trouble getting started, swipe your flat iron over the hair several times to heat and soften the fibers. Backcombing warm hair will result in significantly more teased fiber.

Over-teasing a wig can result in a kinked hair texture

  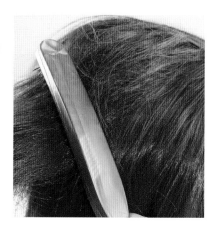

② Hold the hair in one hand toward the hair ends and pinch a small portion of hair between your thumb and forefinger for an added grip.

③ Place your teasing comb or brush onto the hair near the roots or wig cap. Push toward the wig cap so that the hair tangles toward the base of the weft track. Repeat several times until the hair is visibly tangled.

④ Move several inches closer to your hand and repeat the above step for this section of hair. Continue until all the hair is tangled.

Perfectly Pointy Spikes

For a perfect point after teasing, I always add a little PVA glue to my spike. Coating the fibers in a transparent glue like tacky glue is a great way to bring the hair to an extremely sharp point. This technique will also add significantly more strength to your style and can help the rest of your spike last through wear and tear, since tacky glue will not fade over time.

Want something a little less permanent? Try a strong styling gel like göt2b Spiking Glue instead!

① Squeeze a half–pea–sized amount of glue onto your forefinger. Do not dilute this glue. Transfer some onto your thumb and then swipe both of your fingers along the last half-inch or so of your spike.

② Smooth the glue and wring out any visible excess.

TIP: Work quickly and don't over-work the glue. Rubbing after it has begun to dry will cause the glue to pill up in ugly white balls and may leave white streaks. If this happens to you, pick them off or apply water to rehydrate the glue.

Medium-Sized Spikes

Materials:

· Wig head
· Base wig
· Additional wefts
· A teasing brush or comb
· A fine toothed comb
· göt2b Freeze Spray
· Tacky glue or göt2b Spiking Glue
· Clips or bobby pins
· Blow dryer

Double wefting provides a great volume increase, but what about spikes that are simply too long to stay upright on their own? Once your spikes reach a length of 3 inches (7 centimeters) or longer, you may notice that those spikes are beginning to droop or that the fiber will not stay clumped together. Saturating your wig in hairspray may help, but this is only a temporary hold and may result in a flat, compressed spike.

For medium spikes like this that are between 3 and 6 inches (7 and 17 centimeters), we'll be combining two techniques: double wefting to provide texture-free volume and a small amount of teasing for added fluff and security. With most of our volume already wefted in, the core of our teasing will focus on the base of the spike.

Is your wig fiber shorter than 3 inches (7 centimeters)? Don't worry: small spikes or natural-looking hairstyles require less extreme methods. If your desired style is short but requires a large number of well-defined spikes, a double-thick wig should provide enough extra volume without the need for extreme teasing. For a small amount of extra lift, gently tease the crown of your wig or follow Heat Styling Basics: Extra Lift (page 25).

① Add additional wefts to your hair following Wefting Hair (page 46). This step is recommended for styles with multiple spikes or for longer wigs. Focus your new additions around the area to be spiked or, for the largest amount of volume, create a double-thick wig (page 51).

For the best results, purchase a wig style that comes with a small amount of teased fiber at the scalp.

② Gather a handful of hair and separate your first spike. If your base wig came with a pre-teased scalp and you do not want to add additional support, skip to step 7; if your wig is not pre-teased, we will add that needed volume ourselves.

③ Thoroughly tease the bottom 1 inch (2.5 centimeters) of your spike and do not worry about over-teasing.

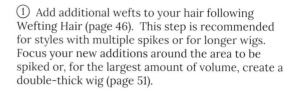

④ Blow dry to lock that new kinked fiber shape in place. Allow to cool, and then comb out the tease. The hair should now be straight but with a slightly more voluminous, kinked texture.

⑤ Add additional teasing to the textured base of the spike, tangling the fibers together so that the spike base holds its shape. Smooth out any over-teased outer fibers with your teasing brush or fine toothed comb. Blow dry and allow to cool.

⑥ If the spike doesn't feel stable or droops too much, comb out the fiber and tease again, repeating this step as many times as necessary.

⑦ The base of your spike should be able to stand on its own, but hairspray will increase this hold and allow you to precisely position the spike. Spritz the spike base with a generous amount of göt2b Freeze Spray. Hold your spike in its desired position and blow dry to set.

Ⓧ Tease a light amount along the remaining length of the spike to solidify the shape and lock the fibers together. Focus on the fiber toward the center of the spike and do not tease too much. The goal for this step is to provide support and not volume.

Continue teasing and combing out the hair until your spike can hold its own shape without drooping.

Ⓧ Run a teasing comb or a fine toothed brush along the outside of the spike in order to smooth out any visibly teased hair.

Ⓧ Mist the entire spike with göt2b Freeze Spray and blow dry to harden. Compress the spike slightly with your hand as you dry to press down any stray fiber.

> TIP: Do not over-saturate your spike in göt2b spray! Instead, be sure to hold the can a foot away and evenly spritz the entire spike. If you accidentally soak the fiber in göt2b, you'll notice that the fiber will separate into "clumps" and stick together.

Ⓧ If desired, follow the instructions for perfectly pointy spikes: squirt a small amount of tacky glue or göt2b Spiking Glue onto your forefinger and thumb. Run your finger along the edge of the spike and allow to set into a point.

Ultimate Teasing: Giant Spikes and Curls

Materials:

· Wig
· Wig head
· Quilting pins
· Teasing brush or comb
· Blow dryer or flat iron
· göt2b Freeze Spray
· Butterfly clips
· Comb

Extreme teasing is not just for spikes! Locking kinked fiber into place provides enough physical support to create fantastic organic shapes such as curls, bulges, or waves. This is an excellent technique to use for the most extreme of hairstyles and one of my favorites, as it gives stylists a large amount of control with a great-looking finished texture.

Giant spikes and large shapes such as curls and bouffant forms require a large amount of teasing in order to create a voluminous understructure, but this can result in unsightly frizz and textured hair. This is not an ideal look when attempting to create a clean finish. However, with a little bit of extra planning we can create an extreme amount of teased understructure volume on the inside while also keeping the top layer of hair slick and smooth.

① Separate a section of fiber to serve as your understructure. Then separate a small amount of hair from all sides of this section and clip it away to save for later. Be sure to save hair from every side of the understructure that will be visible. This saved hair will provide a smooth cover for our teased shape, so be sure to set aside enough fiber to completely cover your understructure.

② Tease the entire section of hair. This first round of teasing will texturize the hair and add volume so do not worry if this tease is very messy. Once teased, heat the hair with a blow dryer or flat iron in order to lock in that new kinked texture. Allow to cool.

③ Comb out the tease and untangle any knots. Your hair should no longer be tangled but will be significantly more voluminous.

④ Repeat the above two steps to tease the hair for a second time. This tease will build on top of the existing fiber kinks to give the hair even more texture and volume. Heat and then comb out the tease.

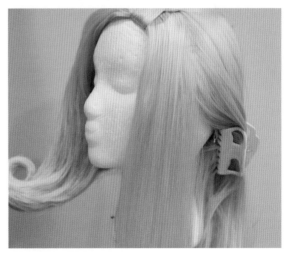

 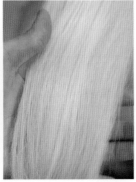

Teased hair texture (*left*) compared to hair that has been teased twice (*right*). Note the increased volume.

(5) The third and final round of teasing will be permanent and will build the physical understructure shape. Begin your teasing at the root of the hair and backcomb until your hair begins to lock together into a solid shape. Be sure to tease the inner layers of the hair first before moving to the outer layers, or else you may have difficulty reaching these inner areas. If the inner areas are hard to reach, switch from a teasing brush to a teasing comb. I love teasing brushes for volume, but a comb is sometimes necessary to penetrate into thick area and lock the fibers together for a better hold.

Extra Tips for Spikes

Compress the hair into a gradual point as you approach the tip. After spraying with göt2b Freeze Spray, press your fibers together and blow dry to compress the hair even more.

Extra Tips for Curls and Shapes

A strong, tangled tease in the center of your shape will be key for achieving extreme curves and turns. Focus on teasing the core into your desired shape, and then add the additional outer hair afterward.

(6) Remember that this tease will be permanent. If you've over-teased and the top layer is looking too ratty, use your teasing brush or a fine toothed comb to comb the top layer of hair back out. A little bit of texture is fine, but if it is too kinked you may have difficulty covering it with smooth hair.

(7) Begin forming your hair into your desired shape as you tease. Tangling the hair while holding it in your desired direction will help it to stay locked in that shape. This may require several rounds of teasing and combing.

(8) Stop teasing once your hair is in roughly the right shape. This shape does not need to be perfect but it should stand on its own: the more physical hold you have, the more permanent your style will be.

TIP: *If you've really done a number on that top layer of hair, try first applying heat from either a steamer or a blow dryer to soften the fiber before combing.*

⑨ Spray generously and evenly with göt2b Freeze Spray, taking care to spritz the inner teased layers as well. At this stage, make sure you address all of your desired details, such as tightening the end of a curl or adjusting the direction of a spike. Tweak your shape until it is positioned correctly, hold in place, and then blow dry to set.

⑩ Unpin the top layer of hair you set aside in step 1. If you had pinned back a large amount of hair, work with only a small amount of fiber at a time, beginning with the wefts closest to the understructure. Working with small amounts will help keep your work clean and will also guarantee that the glue spray saturates all of the hair fibers. Spray your textured shape with göt2b Freeze Spray and then evenly arrange your smooth hair over it in order to cover some of the texture. Spray the smooth hair with göt2b Freeze Spray and blow dry to set.

⑪ Repeat this step for the other small sections in your unpinned layer of hair, continuing to cover the top of your shape until all of the textured hair is hidden.

⑫ Repeat steps 10 and 11 for all sides of your shape, using all of your reserved fiber until the textured hair is covered.

⑬ If your shape comes to a spiked point, follow Perfectly Pointy Spikes (page 60).

Fluffed and Volumized Hair

Materials:

- Wig
- Second wig or purchased wefts
- Wig head
- Quilting pins
- Teasing comb or brush
- Blow dryer or flat iron
- Butterfly or duckbill clips
- göt2b Freeze Spray
- Comb

Teasing can also deliver pure volume for characters with fluffy or extreme hair! This technique works best for layered styles or for wigs shorter than 30 inches (75 centimeters). The longer a wig is, the more teasing or base hair will be required in order to create volume toward the tips, which can result in unsightly frizz.

Like our extreme spikes and curls, extreme volume places most of the textured fiber out of sight within the inner layers of hair, with smoother fiber left visible toward the outside of the wig.

① As an optional step, follow the directions in Double-Thick Wigs (page 51) using a spare harvest wig or additional fibers. This step may be skipped for shorter wigs.

② Clip away the outermost visible layers of hair. Be sure to include the top, bottom, and sides. One-third to one-half of the hair should be clipped aside, exposing only the innermost tracks of fiber.

③ Tease the inner hair. Once teased, heat the hair with a blow dryer or flat iron in order to lock in the new kinked texture. Allow to cool.

④ Comb out the tease and untangle any knots.

⑤ Repeat steps 3 and 4 to add additional volume.

When adding additional texture, focus only on the fiber in the center of your teased area. Over-teasing the outer fiber could result in visible frizz or textured hair, even after covering it with your smooth outer fiber.

⑥ Spritz the teased area with either göt2b or hair-spray. Unclip the pinned portions of hair and style as needed.

GLUEWORK AND FOAMWORK

08

For the most permanent hold and cleanest finish, gluework and foamwork can't be beat! While this technique is more suited to cartoony and unnatural styles, it's the best option for tackling gravity-defying shapes that will stand the test of time. Gluework is a test of patience and can take some getting used to, but mastering it will result in unbelievably clean wigwork.

Types of Understructure

The material you craft your understructure from will depend on two things: first, what shape you are creating, and second, what material you are comfortable working with. Many different materials can be used for the same shape, so always choose what is right for you, so long as it is a lightweight material that does not add large amounts of weight to your wig. This item should also provide a smooth, solid surface for your hair to lie against and should able to be glued or sewn to your base wig. If you are new to foamwork or are struggling with gluing your fiber to the structure, look for a material that is more absorbent such as poster board or felt. It is also possible to cover a less absorbent material in a more absorbent one for better gripping power, for instance covering a foam shape in felt sheets.

If you are looking for some guidance, consider these basics:

Flat spikes or flat objects
Poster board, stiffened felt, or EVA foam

Large spikes
Stiffened felt, Styrofoam, or other foams

Tubes or horns
Foam clay or pre-shaped Styrofoam

Drill curls
Wire and felt

Buns or odango
Styrofoam balls

Extra large ponytails
Styrofoam or batting

Extra large braids
Batting

Complex objects
Foam clay or foams that can be carved

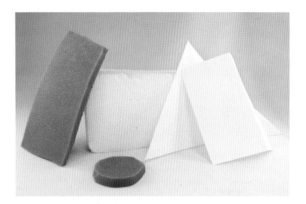

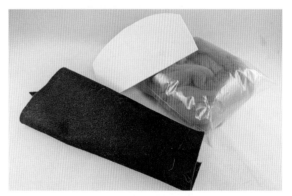

Attaching Your Understructure

Whenever possible, attach your understructure directly to the wig cap or wig netting for added security. Hot gluing the bottom of your structure directly to the wig cap provides a surprisingly strong hold, one which often does not need to be reinforced through extra hand sewing Avoid gluing your understructure on top of your wig's hair fiber, especially if using a long or thick wig. This will not provide a solid base. As the hair moves and shifts, so will your understructure.

If you plan to glue loose or additional fiber to your understructure, be sure to do so before attaching your structure to your wig for an extra clean look. By planning ahead you can glue the edges of the fiber to the underside of the structure, where it will be hidden from view once attached.

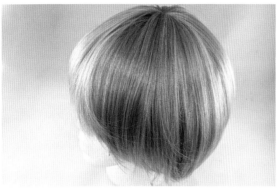

① While wearing your wig, place the understructure in the area you would like it to eventually attach to. Make sure that the understructure base is curved to match your head. If your understructure base is too flat or feels uncomfortable, carve or reform the base until it fits snugly against the curve of your skull.

② Mark the place where the understructure will lie, using clips, bobby pins, or a marker. Remove your wig and place it on your wig head.

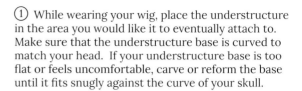

③ Follow the instructions in De-wefting and Harvesting Wefts (page 44) and remove the wefts from this area, exposing the wig netting.

④ If your understructure will attach to the crown, skip to step 5. If it attaches to the sides or lower areas of the wig where the elastic is located, give your structure additional surface area to grip to by adding a piece of felt to this spot. Cut a piece of felt to match the size of your de-wefted area, place it behind the elastic bands, and then sew or glue it to the bands. For added security, use a large piece of felt that extends beyond the de-wefted area.

⑤ Add a generous amount of hot glue to the base of your understructure. Press it into the de-wefted area and hold for several minutes until fully set.

⑥ If desired, sew several reinforcing stitches between the understructure and the wig cap.

Glues for Foamwork

Tacky glue, PVA glue, Pattex Contact Adhesive, and göt2b Freeze Spray are my favorite glues to use for foamwork projects. You can find additional information about each of these glues in Choosing a Glue for Your Project (page 14), but each of these glues dry clear and are useful for different aspects of foamwork. When working with glue, remember to always follow the manufacturer's safety instructions.

Tacky Glue or PVA Glue

This is my foamwork glue of choice because it is versatile, forgiving, and strong. Tacky glue must be diluted with water for a mixture of 1 part water to 3–4 parts glue. Properly prepared glue should have the consistency of thick pancake batter, and remember to rehydrate your glue as the water evaporates.

Hair wefts may be dipped into the glue mixture, or the glue may be painted onto both sides of a weft with a paintbrush. To evenly distribute the glue throughout the fiber and wring out any excess, place your finger against the weft and slide it from the weft track to hair tip, pushing the glue along. This will coat all hair fibers in a thin, clear layer of glue, which will create an extremely permanent hold once dry. You have several minutes to comb, adjust, and arrange correctly diluted tacky glue before it begins to set, which is excellent for creating a clean finish.

If your glue begins to dry, do not touch it, as this will result in pilling and white chunks of glue. If this happens, try adding water to rehydrate it, or pick off or color over any visible flecks once dry.

Pattex Contact Adhesive

For small areas or projects where dry time is important, Pattex Contact Adhesive is a useful alternative to PVA glue. Pattex Contact Adhesive is thinner and more gel-like than PVA glue, and does not require watering down in order to slide it through wig fiber. Pattex Contact Adhesive is more transparent than tacky glue, but it is easy to use an excess amount of glue, leaving a shiny quality to your finished fibers. Rehydrating glue that has begun to dry and pill is even easier: just add water or more Pattex

Contact Adhesive to turn the fiber transparent again. However, Pattex Contact Adhesive dries significantly quicker than white glue and will begin to set within 60 seconds. This makes it ideal for small, fast areas but difficult to use on longer hair or complicated projects that will begin to dry before your styling is complete.

göt2b Freeze Spray

göt2b is not a permanent glue but can still be used to attach wig fiber to foam or other understructure materials so long as you work in thin layers in order to cover each strand of hair. Be more cautious when handling wigs styled with göt2b, as this glue can lose its hold over time and may need to be touched up after transport.

Flat Shapes

If you're a beginner looking for your first foamwork project, a flat understructure is a perfect starting place! Flat or gently curved shapes such as leaves, petals, and fins allow you to work with gravity and do not require any difficult tension or pulling. Your main objective will be to make sure that your wig fiber is correctly coated in glue before arranging the hair in clean lines to completely cover your understructure.

Materials:

· Foam, poster board, or understructure material of choice
· Spare wefts
· Tacky glue, PVA glue, or Pattex Contact Adhesive
· Paintbrush and paint
· Fine toothed comb
· Wax paper
· Scissors

① Construct a base shape from your understructure material. Try to make your shape as smooth as possible and avoid any bumps or ridges. Lay a piece of wax paper onto your workspace and place the understructure on top.

② Paint your shape to match your weft color and allow to dry.

③ Select your glue and dilute with water if needed. Apply a thin line of glue onto your understructure, along where you will lay your first section of hair.

④ Cut a 2-inch (5-centimeter) long weft from your weft pack and then fold it into thirds. Do not cut the hair from the weft track. I highly recommend keeping the hair attached to your weft for now so that you can pull on the fibers without them tangling or pulling away.

> TIP: *More glue is better than less glue. With too little, your glue may begin to dry before you finish coating the fibers, which will cause pilling and an unclear finish.*

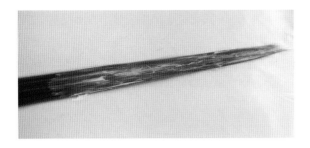

⑤ Comb the hair so that it's free of tangles and then place it onto the wax paper. Paint a generous layer of glue onto the top side.

⑥ Flip the weft and paint a layer of glue onto the other side. Do not worry about adding too much glue.

⑦ With the weft still on the wax paper, hold the weft track steady with one hand. With your other hand, push your finger against the weft hair and slide it from weft track to hair tip. This will infuse the glue throughout the fiber, wringing out any excess while also pressing the hair into a thin layer. Make sure everything is coated in glue and repeat.

If the hair becomes tangled, run a fine toothed comb through the fiber.

⑧ Lay your hair on top of the glued area of the understructure, with both the bottom and top of the weft extending past the understructure base. If the edge of your hair will be visible, take care to form it into a clean point.

⑨ Repeat steps 4–8 for your next row of hair, laying it alongside your first. Continue until your entire base shape is completely covered.

⑩ If your hair is not clinging to the understructure, push the hair into place and apply heat from a blow dryer to quickly dry a portion of the glue. Alternatively, add a duckbill clip or bobby pin to pin it in place while it dries.

⑪ Once dry, cut off the weft tracks that extend beyond the understructure and trim any edges.

Complex Shapes

The technique for covering rounded understructures is very similar to applying fiber to flat shapes. We will still be laying glue-saturated wefts over our understructure but with an extra focus on hiding the weft edges and arranging the fiber around curves. Covering rounded shapes is a more advanced project as it requires fighting against gravity or forcing the hair to bend in an unnatural direction. This can require tugging on the fiber in order to hug a curve, and so it is important to work carefully or secure one end of your fiber to prevent tangling. The following instructions work great for dimensional shapes such as buns, rolls, tubes, foam spikes, fins, and any other understructure that possesses an obvious base.

The direction in which your fiber lies over your rounded understructure can also affect the difficulty and cleanliness of your project. Whenever possible, arrange your fiber in order to hide raw weft edges underneath the understructure where it will eventually attach to your base wig. This is a great trick to create a cleaner look. In addition those weft tracks will be hidden from view, so you can attach them with a stronger but messier glue to help keep them affixed while wrapping the hair.

Below are two ways to wrap a hair bun:

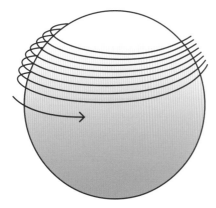

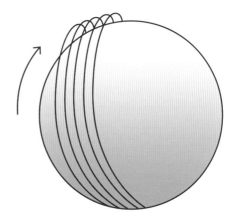

Option 1: Horizontal wrapping. This is a difficult option since the glued area and raw weft edges will be exposed. Wrapping in this fashion might look visibly messy unless you hide that glued edge.

Option 2: Top-to-bottom wrapping. The ability to glue both weft edges to the hidden base of the bun makes this a better choice. With the weft edge secured, you can wrap the fiber around the top of the bun and back down to the underside.

Materials:

- Foam or understructure material of choice
- Spare wefts
- Tacky glue, PVA glue, or Pattex Contact Adhesive
- Blow dryer
- Paintbrush and paint
- Fine toothed comb
- Wax paper
- Hot glue

① Construct a base shape from your understructure material. If possible, choose an absorbent material that your glue will stick to. Lay a piece of wax paper on your workspace and place the understructure on top.

② If desired, paint your shape to match your weft color and allow to dry.

③ Cut a 2-inch (5-centimeter) long weft from your weft pack and then fold it into thirds. Do not cut the hair from the weft track.

④ Squeeze a generous line of hot glue along the weft track and hair fiber. Press the track into the bottom base of the understructure, several millimeters away from the visible edge. The track should be parallel to the edge, with the hair in the direction you wish to wrap it. Feel free to use PVA glue for this step if you wish, but be sure to give it enough drying time.

⑤ Comb the attached hair weft so that it's free of tangles. Dilute your glue with water if needed, and paint a generous layer onto the top side of the weft. Flip the weft and understructure over and paint a second layer of glue onto the new side. Do not worry about adding too much glue.

⑥ With the weft still on the wax paper, hold the weft track steady with one hand. With your other hand, push your finger against the weft hair and slide it from weft track to hair tip. This will infuse the glue throughout the fiber, wringing out any excess glue while also pressing the hair into a thin layer. Make sure everything is coated in glue and repeat. Comb through if the hair becomes tangled.

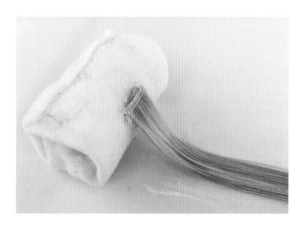

⑦ Apply a thin line of glue onto your understructure, beginning near where you have glued the hair.

⑧ Wrap your hair over the understructure along your glue line. Keep a firm grip and tug if necessary in order to keep the hair flat and smooth around the curve. You may also comb the hair and flatten with your finger if you need more pressure.

⑨ If you are wrapping a round object like a bun or a loop, stop wrapping once you have reached the bottom of the understructure once again. Squeeze a small pool of glue into the base and place the hair over it. Add additional glue on top of the hair press firmly into the fiber with the nozzle of the glue gun. Trim away any excess hair.

⑩ If you are wrapping an object where the edges of the fiber will be visible, trim away any excess hair and add additional glue to the tips of needed. Press the edges firmly against your object. Hold in place with a pin or comb tail and blow dry to set.

⑪ Repeat steps 3–10 for your next row of hair, laying it alongside your first. Continue until your entire base shape is completely covered.

Covering Glued Hair Edges

If your hair wefts cannot be hidden under the base of your understructure, it may be necessary to cover any unsightly edges with an additional layer of hair. Because those edges will be visible, try to work as cleanly as possible or utilize clear PVA glue whenever possible.

Materials:

· Spare wefts
· Tacky glue, PVA glue, or Pattex Contact Adhesive
· Paintbrush
· Fine toothed comb
· Scissors
· Hot glue (optional)

① Choose where your weft edges will fall on your understructure. This should typically be toward the back of your wig where it will be seen less.

② Follow the instructions in Complex Shapes (page 76), but lay the starting edge of your weft at this line. For advanced wig stylists who are feeling confident, try to remove the weft track from your fiber and forgo hot glue, as this will result in a much cleaner finish. Instead, squeeze your PVA glue throughout the fiber and then cut away the weft track.

③ After your hair has dried, trim away any excess fiber at this edge line so that you are left with a straight, blunt line of fiber.

④ Apply a layer of tacky glue over the dried hair on the edge line.

⑤ Cut a 2-inch (5-centimeter) long weft from your weft pack and then fold it into thirds. Apply tacky glue to both sides of this weft and squeeze out any excess.

⑥ Lay the weft over the edge line so that any jagged areas are covered. Allow to dry and trim any excess fiber.

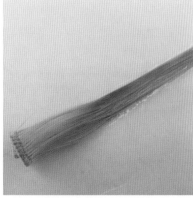

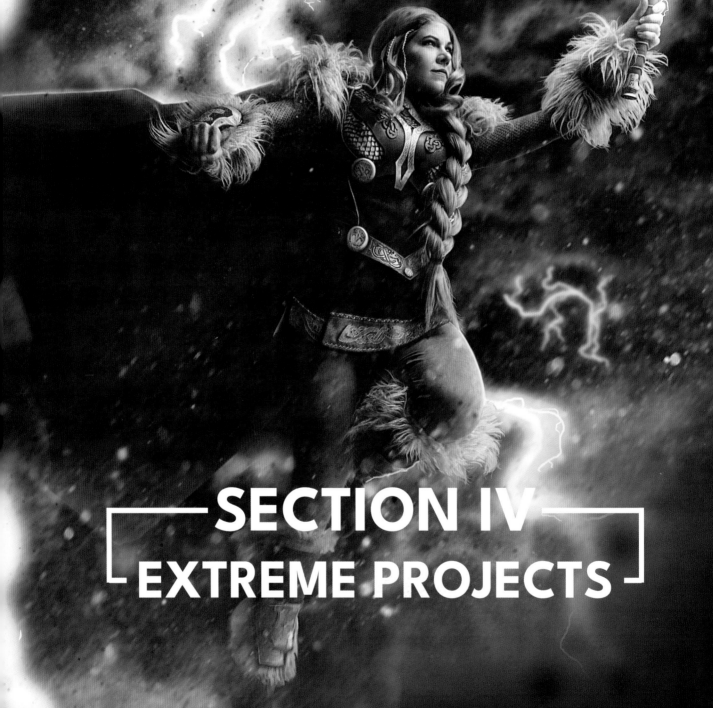

SECTION IV
EXTREME PROJECTS

PROJECT I:
DUAL-TONED
WIGS

Splitting and then combining wigs is an easy way to create a style with two different, distinct color tones! This can be used to create wigs that have a distinct left-right color side, wigs that are split with two different colors on the top and bottom of the wig, or wigs that are color split in other ways. Rather than sewing in extra wefts of a contrasting color, which can be tedious, we'll instead cut apart two different wigs and then sew them together to form a single, dual-toned wig.

With this technique, always remember that we are aiming to reassemble our wigs into the same-sized shape as each wig started in: the cap size of our completed wig should ideally not be larger, smaller, or warped in any way that might make fitting more difficult. For the easiest combination, try to start with two wigs that are the same brand and style. However, you can combine two different styles of wigs, provided that you are careful about matching cut lines and hiding any exposed wefts.

Materials:

· Wig in color 1
· Wig in color 2
· Wig head
· Quilting pins
· Needle and thread
· Marker
· Scissors
· Bobby pins or clips (optional)

① Begin with two different wigs in your two chosen colors. For this example we are creating a wig with silver bangs and a small amount of silver in the front, while the remainder of the wig remains grey.

② Determine where you would like your contrasting color to begin. Mark this line on your first wig with bobby pins or clips. Flip your wig inside out.

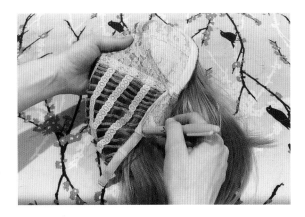

③ Use a marker to draw along the marked line, extending from one edge of the wig to the other. Make sure that your line traces along a structural portion of the wig cap, such as the crown netting, the ear tab, or a piece of elastic. Avoid marking your split line across wefts that are exposed between the elastics, as it will be difficult to sew these individual wefts together when it comes time to combine your wig.

④ Flip your second wig inside out and trace a matching cut line. If using a different style of wig, try to match this line as best you can to the cut line in step 3.

⑤ On both wigs, use scissors to cut along this split line in areas where it meets the edge of the wig, ear tabs, or crown netting. Try to avoid cutting any hair and when in doubt push any excess hair toward the side of the wig you intend to use. If your cut line follows along an elastic band, do not worry about cutting this area.

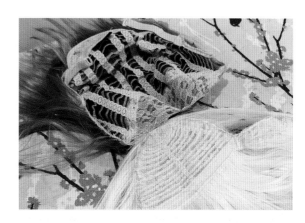

⑥ Set aside the portion of each wig that you do not intend to use. You should now have two different-colored wig halves.

⑦ Align each of these wig halves along the cut line and pin in place. Use a needle and thread to whip-stitch along this line, binding the two wig halves together.

⑧ Flip your combined wig inside out. Depending on your cut line and if you combined two different wigs, you may find that some wefts are too exposed. If this is the case, remove two or three wefts from your discarded wig half and add them over the exposed area.

PROJECT II:
WAVY SPIKES

Wavy spikes are created using the same technique as our moderate spikes (see Medium-Sized Spikes, page 61)—but with a twist! A little bit of extra twisting at the end gives these spikes a fun, interesting look.

Materials:

· Wig
· Wig head
· Teasing comb or brush
· Blow dryer
· Flat iron
· Fine tooth comb
· göt2b Freeze Spray
· PVA glue or göt2b Spiking Glue

① Separate a handful of hair and tease both the base and body of the spike. Try to focus most of your teasing on the base hair in order to hold your spike together while leaving the visible hair smooth.

② Smooth out any visibly over-teased hair using your teasing brush or comb.

③ Continue teasing and smoothing until the spike can stand on its own.

④ Use a flat iron to heat the body of the spike until the hair is limp. A blow dryer may be used instead but it will require more effort to heat the spike to the correct temperature.

⑤ Use your fingers to arrange the fiber into a wave. Hold until completely cool.

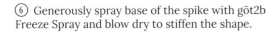

⑥ Generously spray base of the spike with göt2b Freeze Spray and blow dry to stiffen the shape.

⑦ Comb the body of the spike to smooth out stray hairs. Spritz with göt2b Freeze Spray and blow dry.

⑧ Apply a clear glue or gel to the spike tip, smoothing it to a point with your fingers.

⑨ Trim away any stray hairs.

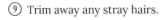

**PROJECT III:
REMOVABLE
HAIR PIECES**

A heavy or unbalanced wig can spell trouble. These types of wigs are difficult to travel with, and the unbalanced weight can pull the entire wig to one side while you are wearing it. For large objects such as oversized ponytails, pigtails, hair loops, or even non-hair objects such as hats, we need a hidden way to both balance and break down these styles.

This technique involves attaching a large headpiece to a headband hidden inside the wig. These two pieces are screwed together and firmly attached through the wig's netting. While invisible, the headband serves two important purposes. First, it redistributes the accessory's weight evenly to the center of the head, which provides significantly more balance and stability. Second, these hair pieces may be unscrewed and re-screwed together for easy transport.

Materials:

- · Wig
- · Hair piece
- · Dremel or other drilling tool
- · Hot glue
- · 1-inch (2.5-centimeter) wide headband
- · Two 1- to 1.5-inch (2.5- to 4-centimeter) screw posts or "Chicago screws"
- · Seam ripper

① Inspect your screw posts. You should have two parts: a small screw and a "post" for the screw to twist into.

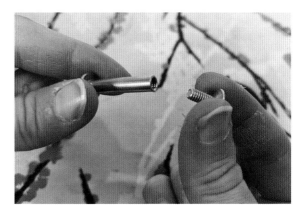

② Place the headband inside the wig. Determine where your hair piece will sit and mark this point on both the headband and wig.

③ Remove the headband from inside the wig and place the headband in a clamp. Drill a hole through the point you made in step 2. Be sure to read and follow the safety information for the drill you are using.

④ Mark the center bottom of your hair piece and hollow out a small hole for your post to fit into. This will work best if your headpiece is made of foam, Styrofoam, foil, or any other solid material.

(5) Fill the hole with glue and insert your post so that the bottom is aligned with the base of your hair piece.

(6) Make sure it is centered and hold in place until the glue sets.

(7) Push the screw through the bottom of the headband hole.

(8) Place the headband inside your wig. Seam rip a small hole in the netting above the screw and push through until the screw is visible.

(9) Arrange the hairpiece so that the screw and post are aligned. Slot together, and twist until tightened. Use a screwdriver for extra security, but stop tightening when you meet resistance or else you risk dislodging the glue.

(10) Unscrew at any time for easy traveling.

PROJECT IV:
FIBER FEATHERS

Fiber feathers require more attention to detail than other similar projects, but the finished effect is quite impressive! These feathers require very little understructure, which means that your feather will look great from all angles. For an extra pop, try blending together multiple fiber colors before beginning.

The trick to a frustration-free feather is to work clean and avoid accidentally shifting the delicate fibers in your workspace with too much air from a blow dryer or hairspray. A pin or the tail end of a comb can also help when trying to precisely move these small fibers.

Materials:

· Wig wefts
· PVA glue or tacky glue
· göt2b Freeze Spray
· Poster board
· Scissors
· Wax Paper
· Paintbrush and paint to match your weft

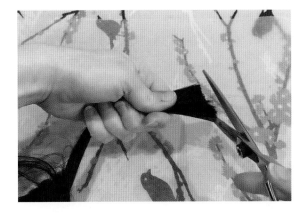

① Remove a handful of weft hair and cut into 1-inch (2.5-centimeter) long pieces.

② Place a piece of wax paper over your work area and arrange the hair pieces in a 5- to 6-inch (12.5- to 15-centimeter) tall line. Align the left side of the pieces so that they form a straight line.

③ Rotate the hair pieces so that they are at a 45 degree angle. Rotate the pieces toward the top of the line more, tilting them more and more upward until they are at a 90 degree angle. This will form the right side of your feather.

④ Spray with göt2b Freeze Spray to temporarily hold the hair in place and allow time to dry. Be sure to hold the can at least a foot away to prevent accidentally blowing your hair around.

⑤ Repeat steps 1–4 for the left side of your feather, laying the hair beside the first side and rotating the hair 45 degrees in the opposite direction.

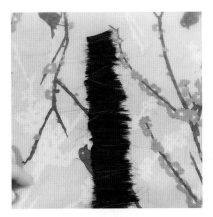

⑥ Carefully slide a spare piece of poster board under your feather. Flip the feather and generously spray with göt2b Freeze Spray. Allow time to dry.

⑦ Paint a generous amount of glue down the center of the feather. This will form the feather's bottom side.

⑧ Cut a strip of poster board that is .25 inches (6 millimeters) wide and half an inch (12 millimeters) shorter than your feather. If desired and if the bottom of your feather will be visible, paint to match your weft color.

⑨ Place the poster board over the line of glue, covering it completely. Allow several hours to dry.

⑩ Flip the feather again and paint a generous amount of glue onto the feather's top side.

⑪ Cut a small amount of weft hair that is 1 inch (2.5 centimeters) longer than the length of your feather. Place over the line of glue.

Allow your feather to completely dry over several hours.

⑫ Once dry, generously spray the top and bottom with göt2b Freeze Spray. Trim either side of your feather into a gentle curve and cut away any uneven or unglued fiber.

PROJECT V:
FIBER SCALES

Scales are fast, lightweight, and give wigs a great textured effect. This gluework is unique in that scales do not require an understructure. Instead, the small size of the scale and the stiffness of the glue provides all the strength it needs to permanently hold its shape.

Materials:

· Wig wefts
· Fine tooth comb
· Pattex Contact Adhesive, tacky glue, or PVA glue
· Scissors
· Duckbill clips
· Wax Paper

Dragon Scales

① Remove a 2- to 3-inch (5- to 8-centimeter) wide weft from your weft pack and fold into thirds.

② Cut the end of your weft an inch (2.5 centimeters) or more longer than your desired scale length. Feather the edge and comb through to smooth out the fibers.

③ Paint a generous amount of clear glue onto both sides of the weft. Comb your weft if any hair becomes tangled.

④ Press your forefinger and thumb onto either side of the weft and press together. Drag your fingers along the weft from the weft track to tip, wringing out any excess glue.

⑤ Place the weft on wax paper. Pinch the hair tip into a point.

⑥ Allow to fully dry over several hours.

⑦ Once hardened, cut to your desired scale size.

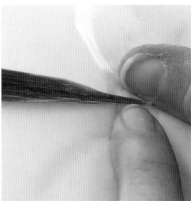

Fish Scales

Fish scales are created in a similar way to dragon scales but with a curved twist. Staggering the scales together is the perfect way to create wig-hair animals like this fiber fish—just glue the bottom of each scale to your understructure as you layer each piece.

① Remove a 2- to 3-inch (5- to 8-centimeter) wide weft from your weft pack and fold into thirds.

② Paint a generous amount of clear glue onto both sides of the weft. Comb your weft if any hair becomes tangled.

③ Press your forefinger and thumb onto either side of the weft and press together. Drag your fingers along the weft from the weft track to tip, wringing out any excess glue.

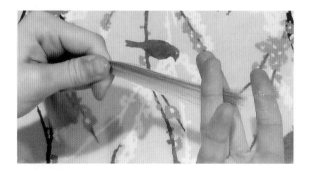

④ Pinch the weft and bend it into a U shape, spreading out the fibers with your free hand.

⑤ Use a strong duckbill clip to clamp the bottom of the U into place. Allow to dry.

⑥ Use scissors to trim off the bottom of the U, as well as any stray fibers.

**PROJECT VI:
FIBER FLOWERS**

I love creating fiber flowers! Flowers come in all shapes and sizes, so there's no limit to how simple or complex your design can become. The key to a foamwork fiber flower is to create multiple petals and overlap them slightly to create a visually interesting structure. Adding gluework leaves and vines will give your flower even more visual interest as well. Tiny vines like these are constructed with just glue and no understructure at all, and if you're feeling ambitious you can even create small petals using this understructure-free technique.

Materials:

- · Wig wefts
- · Poster board
- · Paintbrush and paint
- · PVA or tacky glue
- · Hot glue
- · Wax paper

- · Scissors
- · Comb
- · Duckbill clip
- · Quilting pins (optional)
- · Foam sheet (optional)

① Determine the petal shape that you would like and cut 5–6 identical copies of this shape from poster board. For a beginner-friendly flower, cut a flat shape for your petal. For a more advanced flower with additional dimension, cut and tape your poster board so that it is curved. Color your shape to match your weft color.

② Remove a small amount of weft hair and feather the tip of the weft. Place it on your wax paper.

③ Paint a generous amount of clear glue onto both sides of the weft. Comb your weft if any hair becomes tangled.

④ Press your finger against the surface of the weft, close to the sewn edge. Slide your finger toward the tail of the weft to smooth down the fibers and wring out excess glue.

⑤ Paint a line of PVA glue along the center of your petal template.

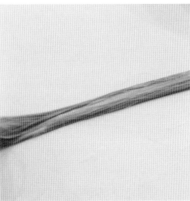

(6) Arrange your weft so that a half-inch of fiber extends past the top tip of the petal template, and place your weft on top of the glue line. If the hair is pulling away from the template, clip it down with a duckbill clip or blow dry to expedite the drying process (see the bottom right photo on page 97).

(7) Repeat steps 2–6 for the next section of hair and place it next to the first. Repeat until your first petal is completely covered. Use additional glue if necessary to bring the hair at the tip of your petal to a clean point.

(8) Repeat steps 2–7 for the remaining petals and allow to dry.

(9) Once dry, trim away any excess fiber from the bottom of your petal.

(10) Arrange your petals in a loose circle so that each petal overlaps slightly. Hot glue the base of each petal to your wig netting or to another surface such as poster board if you would like to attach your flower later.

(11) Add some extra visual interest to your flower by creating optional vines. To prep your space, place a piece of wax paper over a piece of foam. Remove a very small quantity of green wefts and generously coat both sides with PVA glue. Pinch your thumb and forefinger together near the sewn weft end and slide your fingers toward the base of the weft.

(12) Place your weft on your wax paper and curve into an S shape. Press quilting pins through the paper and into the foam to brace your hair and keep it in place as it dries.

(13) Once completely dry, the stiffened glue should be strong enough to hold this thin hair in its shape without the need for an understructure. Trim away excess hair and artistically arrange around your flower before gluing in place.

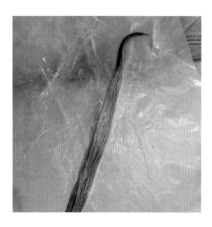
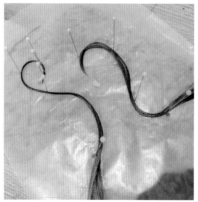

Creating a basket weave or harlequin pattern from wig fiber is an amazing way to add a complex-looking pattern to your wig. This technique utilizes gluework, which results in an extremely sturdy and very clean finished look. Once completed you can attach your finished basket or harlequin pattern to your wig using either a needle and thread or hot glue.

Materials:

- Wig Wefts
- A contrasting wig weft color for a harlequin pattern
- Fine toothed comb
- Tacky glue or PVA glue
- Scissors
- Masking tape
- Poster board
- Markers
- Wax paper
- Paintbrush and paint

① Determine the size you would like your completed pattern to be, and sketch that desired shape onto poster board. Draw your basket weave or harlequin pattern onto this template, angling your lines to form a repeating pattern of diamonds or squares.

② Remove a small portion of your first weft color. Fold until you have a layer of 5–6 wefts.

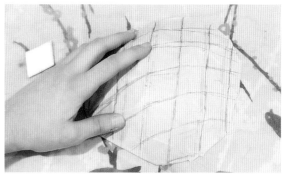

③ Paint a generous amount of clear glue onto both sides of the weft. Comb your weft if any hair becomes tangled.

④ Press your finger against the surface of the weft, close to the sewn edge. Slide your finger toward the tail of the weft to smooth down the fibers and wring out excess glue.

⑤ Arrange your weft on the template so that it lies between the two centermost lines. Gently manipulate the weft strip around any curves. If your surface is rounded or the hair is pulling away from the template, tape the strip's edges to the wax paper or blow dry to expedite the drying process.

⑥ Repeat steps 2–5 for your second weft strip and place it beside the first strip, between the next two guidelines. Repeat this process for all remaining parallel stripes.

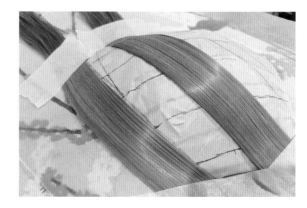

(7) Allow to dry for 1–2 hours, until the strips are partially dry but still flexible. Once dry, remove your tape and place the weft strips aside for later.

(8) Repeat steps 2–7 using a contrasting weft color for the strips if creating a harlequin pattern; for a basket weave the same color may be used. This time place the weft strips between the lines that run in a perpendicular direction to the previous strips and allow 1 hour of dry time.

(9) Weave one of your original strips back and forth through the strips that are currently drying on the template. Position the strip until it is close to its original position on the template.

(10) Select the next contrasting strip and weave it in opposition to the previous strip to create an alternating pattern. Slide the strip down and align with the template. Repeat until all strips are woven together.

(11) Gently compress and tighten the strips until your desired pattern emerges.

(12) Press all edges down with tape if needed and allow to fully dry overnight. Once dry, remove the tape and template, and cut away any excess fiber. Your pattern is now ready to attach to your wig.

Additional Resources

Buying Guide

Arda Wigs
arda-wigs.com

Arda Wigs Canada
ardawigscanada.ca

Arda Wigs Europe
arda-wigs.eu

Epic Cosplay
epiccosplay.com

Coscraft
coscraft.co.uk

The Five Wits
thefivewitswigs.com

Dye Manufacturers

Rit Dye
ritdye.com

iDye and Jacquard Products
jacquardproducts.com

Additional Reading

Wigs 101 and *Wigs² – Level Up*, by Kukkii-San
wigs101.com

Wig Styling for Cosplay, by Kinpatsu Cosplay
kinpatsucosplay.com

About the Author

Regan Cerato is one-half of Cowbutt Crunchies Cosplay, an internationally acclaimed couple who specializes in complex couture cosplay and incredible pop culture–based designs. Crowned as the Global Champion of Cosplay in 2019, Regan is a passionate craftsperson who is always pushing the envelope of cosplay to create new and more innovative outfits. She and her wife's love of cosplay has taken them around the world, judging contests and hosting workshops everywhere from at home in New England to Sydney, Australia. With twenty years of experience, their focus is on learning, creativity, and introducing newcomers to the art of cosplay.

You can find more of their work at cowbuttcrunchiescosplay.com.

Want even more creative content?

Visit us online at ctpub.com

FREE PATTERNS | FREE VIDEO TUTORIALS | TOOLS | GIFTS & MORE!

sew
snap
share

f y t ▶ ⊙ P